Stalking Big Game

Stalking Big Game

Walt Prothero

STACKPOLE
BOOKS

Published by
STACKPOLE BOOKS
Cameron and Kelker Streets
P.O. Box 1831
Harrisburg, PA 17105

Cover photo by Walt Prothero

Cover design by Mark B. Olszewski

Interior layout by Margaret N. Schmidt

Interior drawings by Walter K. Prothero

Printed in the United States of America

First Edition

10 9 8 7 6 5 4 3 2 1

Library of Congress Cataloging-in-Publication Data

Prothero, Walter L.
    Stalking big game / Walter L. Prothero.
        p.   cm.
    Includes index.
    ISBN 0-8117-0282-0
    1. Big game hunting.   I. Title.
    SK33.P77   1992
    799.2'6 — dc20   92-754
                                                                                     CIP

Dedicated
to
Cheri, Mom, and Dad

Contents

Acknowledgments

To Cheri Flory, for photographic and paperwork assistance, for sharing campfires from well below the equator to well north of the Arctic Circle, and for her encouragement and enthusiasm in writing this book, I owe more than just a debt of gratitude. I also wish to express thanks to my dad, Walter K. P., for the illustrations that so well grace the pages of this volume.

I also wish to thank Judith Stolz, former editor at Stackpole, for recruiting me to write this, Mary McGinnis, and John Cominsky for their advice and support.

Thanks also to the best guides, who always give you something more than game: to Willie Phillips of Maun, Botswana, for showing me on foot a primeval and pristine part of Africa I thought no longer existed; to Ralph Kitchen, top Stone sheep guide, for those sixteen-hour days pursuing rams; and to Russell Tarr, ace Zimbabwe professional hunter, for his keenness and enthusiasm in the chase.

Thanks also to all the native guides: Charlie and Herbie, Shuswap Indians in British Columbia, who risked their lives dodging avalanches while pursuing my trophy goat; Joseph, a Bayei, and Patrick, a Bushman, in the Okavango, for their tracking and persistence; and

Luka, Shorty, and Matchapitza, trackers and Matabele hunters, who could read spoor in that Zimbabwe bush like no one else in the world. They taught me what could be done and what to strive for. I expect, too, that I'll be striving only to approximate their kind of perfection the rest of my life. But at least it gives me something to shoot for.

And last, thanks to all the hunters I've shared campfires with, especially Richard Lovell, who has hunted with me from Colorado to above the Arctic Circle. And to Sam Rick and Rick Lowe, good luck.

Preface

When Judith Stolz, then an editor at Stackpole, recruited me to write a book on stalking back in early 1990, I was afraid she wanted one on the narrow definition of stalking—that is, what you do to close the distance *after* game is sighted. It would be tough to write a "how-to" book only on that, and I told her so. But she had in mind a book on hunting, really; in other words, she wanted a book on the broad definition of stalking—everything you do to hunt big game (excluding motor vehicles, of course), including still hunting, tracking, brushing, and ambushing, as well as closing the distance once game is sighted. This book uses that broader definition and is written not only in explanatory exposition but also with liberal use of hunting anecdotes to illustrate various points. In writing for magazines, I find I get more letters in response to articles that are anecdotal and narrative in form. Hunters like hunting stories (if you think they don't, just put two or more of them together for any length of time), and they like them more than instructions.

This book is divided into habitat types: plains game, forest and savanna game, and mountain game. The habitat type an animal is found in determines how you stalk it even more than the animal itself. Some species, such as mule deer, may inhabit more than one type of habitat. Because hunting them in each type requires different tactics, they have their own chapters in each part. Other species are restricted to one habitat type: mountain sheep and goats live in the mountains, and pronghorn antelope are creatures of the plains.

Ninety-eight percent of my hunting has been done without the aid of guides, so I couldn't rely on someone else's knowledge if I was going to secure a trophy. The only time I've used guides was when it was required by law, as in Canada and Africa. I've hunted in Saskatchewan, Alberta, British Columbia, Zimbabwe, and Botswana with guides. I think hunting without guides is the best way—it forces the hunter to learn and become a better naturalist and woodsman. Similarly, if you go it solo you're less distracted by companions. You notice important clues and information while stalking that otherwise would be missed, since you spend less time interacting with another and more time looking for sign. When hunting alone, you keep aware of wind direction, listen, and search for the quarry. Besides that, guides are expensive, with fees sometimes reaching one thousand dollars per day!

To some of us, we do more than live to hunt; we hunt to live. Hunting is something that is firmly entrenched on a dominant gene deep in the double-helix maze of our DNA. Some of us, too, hunt for more than game; we stalk for meaning. If I'm out of whack with the world, if I'm frustrated by the red tape that's an inevitable part of surviving in this society, if I'm fed up with checkbooks and taxes, with teaching and writing, I stalk game to become synchronized again, both with myself and the rest of the world. My annual expeditions into the northern wilderness are more than hunting trips. They allow me to put things into perspective and strengthen my tolerance so I can handle civilization the rest of the year. Though they don't vocalize it, I find the same thing in many of my hunting chums.

During the off-season when I can't hunt, I must read and talk about it. I like nothing better than having Russell Tarr, top Zimbabwe professional hunter, visit during the winter and regale me with safari stories. I also exchange letters and photos with guides, outfitters, editors, and any number of friends from California to New Hampshire and Africa to Alaska. That's an important part of my off-season— that and reading hunting books. One of my major expenses during the winter is buying hunting books, and if you can get a fraction of the satisfaction out of this volume that I've gotten out of *Sheep and Sheep Hunting, Hunter, Man-Eaters of India, The Green Hills of Africa, Bell of Africa, Meditations on Hunting,* or any of dozens of others, then my labors will have been much more than sufficiently rewarded.

Part I
Plains Game

Tracking, and to a lesser extent still hunting, is of less importance in hunting animals on bare, open plains and prairies. Usually hunters locate game from a distance, often with binoculars or a spotting scope, and stalk by staying out of sight. Plains game generally relies on vision to detect potential danger, and usually, though not always, on fleeing to escape it.

When sneaking up on plains game, less consideration is given to wind direction, since tricky and erratic winds scatter scents far and wide on open prairies. The actual sneak often begins a great distance away from the quarry, so wind direction is likely to be out of a different quarter. Also, less thought is given to hunter noise and "quiet" clothing such as wool isn't as important as in the woods, where a branch scraping against stiff fabric can give a hunter away at a quarter mile. Frequently, shooting is done at longer ranges—at two hundred, three hundred, and even four hundred yards (though that *is* a bit far!)—and the hunter never really has to consider wind direction or whether his pants are scraping brush or his boots grating the rocks. Just the same, sometimes the sneak can put a hunter much closer to game, and then wind direction and hunter noise do become important considerations.

Animals that have inhabited the plains for millennia have evolved eyesight that's phenomenal. So if you're after an old pronghorn buck that's been chivied much, he'll act on what he sees. Veteran bucks have an uncanny ability to stay just out of rifle range. That's how they got old and big. The same can be said for southern African gemsbok. They'll keep six or seven hundred yards between you and them, and if you try to narrow the distance, they'll move off across the dry pan or desert until they feel safe again. Gemsbok have survived tens of thousands of years with lions, wild hunting dogs, hyenas, and Bushman as predators.

Getting up on a quarry in the open requires staying out of sight, and if there's no cover, hunting becomes frustrating business. (Unlike pronghorn antelope, gemsbok sometimes live in thick savannas, too, and getting a shot there isn't such a trick.) Since there's little or no vegetation over a foot or two high, staying hidden sometimes means crouching and skulking along gullies or ravines, slithering through cacti, scorpions, or rattlesnakes, and soiling those stylish Abercrombie & Fitch safari clothes. It often requires long, extended stalks, sometimes lasting an entire day. Poking your head out of cover and glassing needs to be done very carefully. It's critical not to tip the quarry with binocular or rifle reflection. In short, sneaking up on plains game requires a classic sneak. And you'll value that pronghorn, prairie mule deer, or barren-ground caribou all the more for the torturous stalk.

1

Pronghorn Antelope

I hunted my first pronghorn antelope in 1964 in the heart of Wyoming's Red Desert. Up to that time, I'd shot a couple of mule deer in mountainous northern Utah, so the alkaline, dusty-white, countertop-flat country was pretty exotic to me. Instead of thick trees where I had hunted deer, the tallest vegetation was wind-stunted, shin-high sagebrush, grasses, and prickly pear cacti. I was fourteen at the time and pretty green. My nearest encounter with antelope hunting had been listening to a couple of neighbors back in Utah bragging about chasing antelope in pickups or potting them by resting the rifle across the hood of the truck at seven hundred yards. I was a bit green, as I said, but I recognized them as blowhards.

So I stepped out of the battered old Willys Jeep that morning and stared at my first herd of antelope. I'd read something (if memory serves it was by Jack O'Connor) about judging antelope trophies—the horn should be as long as the chest is deep, there should be a prominent hook, and so on—and from what I'd memorized, the herd buck was a good one. But there wasn't enough cover to conceal a large jackrabbit, and the antelope were four hundred yards away watching me, though they weren't especially alarmed. The sun was rising above my shoulder and blazing into the antelope's eyes, so I reasoned that perhaps they wouldn't be able to make me out. Actually, that was more wishful hoping than solid reasoning. My sneak in the end consisted of walking toward them with the sun in their eyes, bent over at the waist and presenting a silhouette of what I hoped would resemble a grazing pronghorn enough to allow me to close the distance a hundred yards or so. It did, probably because the pronghorn in those days were pretty innocent about the evil habits of men. I killed that buck with a single shot at something just over three hundred yards, and I must have set some sort of record for the three-hundred-yard dash over sagebrush and cacti. He measured just 14¾ inches, and I clearly remember panting up to him and smelling his musky pungency and marveling at his harlequin marking. In spite of a crude stalk, I had managed to collect that buck largely because he was naive. Today it's tough to imagine sneaking up on a good buck during hunting season in the open.

But the sneak is what makes antelope hunting exciting. Pronghorn country consists mostly of prairies—from incredibly flat places in parts of the Red Desert, to rolling hills cut by gullies and ravines in western Wyoming and much of Montana, to rolling and sometimes brushy lands with scattered trees in other places. In general, though, the best hunting and biggest bucks come from very flat country like Wyoming's Red Desert. Such country requires the most finesse and concentration in pulling off the sneak.

Animals that have evolved in flat country rely mostly on eyesight to detect danger. The pronghorn is no exception. In fact, it has the best sight of any animal I've hunted, including mule deer, mountain sheep, and several African plains antelope. Stalking man-wise bucks these days requires staying out of sight in very flat country, which is difficult. You have to keep low, often slithering on your belly, and use every bit of cover available. You have to be careful about binocular or rifle reflection. In spite of flat terrain, there are sometimes shallow ravines and erosion rills running across the land. Some of these are deep enough to allow you to close quickly by sprinting up them in a crouch. This kind of sneak is an exciting, adrenaline-pumping business.

Once an antelope has picked you up and knows you're up to no good, he relies on his incredible speed to get out of your vicinity. Speed has worked for millennia to outrun team-hunting prairie wolves (now extinct in the United States) and coyotes, as well as primitive and modern man.

Doe pronghorns drop fawns late in the spring, in May and June, and before long the young are up and about and able to sprint with adults should the need arise. Rutting (breeding) occurs in September, peaking about the end of the month. Most rutting has pretty well ended by October. Pronghorns are unusual among animals that possess horns in that they annually shed the horn sheath not long after the rut, usually by November. For a while, the light-colored bony core is obvious. But hairs soon coalesce around the core and turn dark, and the horns continue to grow for the rest of the year.

Buck pronghorns typically are territorial beasts, establishing territories in March or April. Bucks three years old or older establish territories up to a mile and a half across. These territories are likely to have feed in September and attract does during the rut. During the spring and summer, younger bucks wandering through the area become aware of the big, aggressive territorial buck and avoid the area. As a result, the big buck, without fighting, establishes dominance. Dominance is critical in establishing territory and attracting does in breeding condition (estrus).

In country where the antelope tend to be territorial, it's a fairly simple matter to locate a good buck's range. All that is required is a bit of preseason scouting. Once you've found a decent buck, watch him. Look for territorial marking places where a buck has pawed out a shallow depression and then urinated and defecated in it. If the buck's there a day or two later, and a week after that, you can be sure that's his territory and he'll be there in September when hunting season opens.

In truth, a couple of sightings in the same area is usually enough confirmation that the buck is in his territory. I prefer to watch him a bit more, however, and determine his favorite bedding areas, feeding sites, hiding places, and watering holes. That way, I'm reasonably sure of finding him anytime I get down to the actual hunting. I much prefer hunting territorial to nonterritorial bucks, because they'll stay in a certain area at least until they lose their territory, and locating them is simpler.

Classic antelope stalking includes glassing and locating the animal, planning the sneak, and sneaking up on the game. Still hunting and tracking *normally* play little part in hunting pronghorns, simply because the country is so open.

Let's go through a classic antelope stalk for the territorial buck, step by step. It's a clear, windy, cold day on Wyoming's high plains. The hunting season is four or five days old, and the antelope have settled at least partially back into their routines after the melee of opening weekend (a state conservation officer once told me that 90

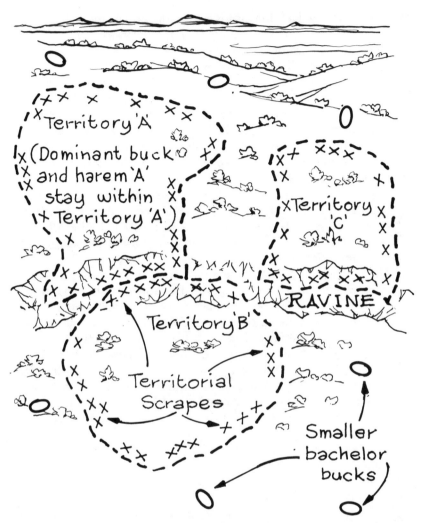

Territory 'A'

(Dominant buck and harem 'A' stay within Territory 'A')

Territory 'C'

RAVINE

Territory 'B'

Territorial Scrapes

Smaller bachelor bucks

Dominant bucks of three years and older establish and maintain territories that are attractive to does, which they defend from other bucks. The most dominant and biggest bucks select the best territories and breed with the most does. Younger, nonterritorial bucks wander the periphery of territories.

percent of all antelope are killed on opening weekend, and most of those on opening day). I'm lying between sagebrushes trying to get out of the wind, slowly scanning with binoculars a buck's territory I'd found in preseason. A doe appears, then another, then a dozen more, and finally the buck shows and profiles on a low, distant rise against the cold, blue sky. He's too far for a shot, of course, and I slither back behind the rise I'm on. The wind is from the north. An autumn storm is intensifying as it slides down the back side of the Rockies, and the herd is to the south half a mile away.

I walk quickly down the ravine behind the rise, then stalk up another larger gully south, then east. The herd is somewhere to the southwest now, and my scent is being scattered out away from them, although there's no danger of them scenting me at more than half a mile. The gully peters out, the rise flattens, and when I stand straight I can see the antelope. I crouch and close, then it's necessary to crawl. I'm glad it's too cold now for rattlesnakes — there are plenty in this country — but I acquire prickly pear spines in various parts of my anatomy. I rise cautiously and see the antelope feeding slowly in my direction. The wind is still favorable, and I notice the herd buck is better than I thought. The sun is behind me, so there's less danger of a giveaway reflection from the binoculars.

Then I crawl more and shorten the distance again. I see a peculiar mound and squirm to it and look over. The antelope are two hundred yards away and closing, so all I have to do is lie still and wait. The wind's still good, blowing off toward Colorado, and the herd is still feeding my way. I carefully place my rolled up jacket in the crotch of a foot-high sagebrush and inch the .270 onto it. Then I prepare myself mentally. I *know* I'll get the buck, and I do — at just over a hundred yards. As with most stalks and sneaks, the shooting was anticlimactic. I collected that trophy buck because I'd earlier found his territory and was pretty sure he'd stay around awhile, and because I stayed out of sight on the sneak.

As the rut progresses, more and more wandering younger bucks are attracted to a dominant buck's territory, because that's where the ladies are. As a result, the harem master is kept busy displaying to outrider bucks (this involves a side display, often accompanied by explosive, wheezy snorts and a series of chugs not unlike an old steam engine), and if that doesn't work, chasing them and possibly even fighting. I once witnessed two bucks in a bloody fight. Both had several gashes in their necks, and one had been hooked up a nostril so badly that he left a clear blood trail along the road for three-quarters of a mile until he turned off. As the rut peaks, in the last part of September, the territorial buck may reduce the size of his territory so it's easier to defend. Also, as a result of pressure from other bucks, the dominant male very frequently moves his harem into hiding someplace within his territory. Ravines, sinks, swales, and gullies are favorite hiding places.

For does, one of the main benefits of associating with a dominant, territorial buck is peace and quiet. Does are therefore quite willing to hide. If you've been watching a territorial buck in the preseason but can't seem to find him during the rut and hunting season, look for hiding places. One of the best bucks I've collected I found in hiding. I still hunted along a low ridge near the center of his territory, and in the third small ravine, I noticed the buck's horns above the curve of the slope. I squirmed through the scant sage and dropped that 16½-inch buck with a single shot at sixty yards right in the center of his harem. He scored after shrinkage 83 Boone-and-Crockett points, enough for listing in their "Bible." But, as Robert Ruark once said about some large African beast he killed, "I couldn't care less."

In an antelope population where there are a number of territories, any buck's territory will probably survive through the rut because a higher proportion of bucks are defending their own, not out challenging herd bucks. In a population where there are many young, non-territorial bucks, a dominant buck is likely to eventually abandon his territory because it becomes impossible to defend by the sheer weight of the other bucks challenging him. Often this happens toward the end of the rut and hunting season and has little real meaning for the hunter. But the higher the proportion of younger bucks in a population, the shorter the time territories will survive during the rut.

Sometimes, due to selective hunting pressure and harvest on trophy bucks, severe winters within the past three years or so, or poor range or water conditions, a buck population may be made up almost entirely of young males. When that's the case, the territorial-defense scheme will shift to a harem-defense strategy, where bucks defend an area around a quite mobile harem. During the mid-1980s, just after the severe winters of '83 and '84, there were virtually no territorial bucks where I hunted in the Red Desert. Older, territorial bucks do most of the breeding and consequently deplete fat reserves. They go into winter in poor condition and are the first to die off. Before those bad winters, the place was almost exclusively made up of big bucks defending territories.

Unfortunately, many places are becoming a harem-defense hunting proposition. I say "unfortunately" because harem defense means fewer really good bucks in excess of 14 inches, and because harem-defense hunting is less productive and predictable. It's been my experience that bucks defending a mobile harem instead of a territory wander more widely, so preseason scouting is of less use in locating a trophy buck. It's quite possible to find several harems in a limited area, and if that's the case, the hunter too often blunders into and frightens one herd while he's making a sneak on another. When you're hunting in a harem-defense area, you'll see fewer really good bucks, if any. You'll spend more time collecting the buck you do get, and even then, it will likely be accidental. And you'll be more at the mercy of Lady Luck, rather than relying on your own skill.

But if you're forced to hunt in a harem-defense scheme, make the most of it. Preseason scouting isn't totally out of the picture, though its emphasis has changed. Instead of locating an individual trophy buck, look for places where antelope hang out. Watch also for concentrations of sign, such as tracks, droppings, cropped brush and grasses, and well-used trails (especially to a watering or feeding area). If you find a place with a reasonably fresh concentration of sign, spend your time hunting there. Often, ambushing is an effective technique (more about this later), particularly along trails to watering or feeding areas. If the country is hilly or there are trees or ravines about, still hunting can be even more effective.

Though big bucks are more scarce in harem-defense country, there may be one or two grandfathers around anyway. Single, old bucks may no longer participate in the goings-on of the rut and will hide in remote basins or hills. If you're after such an old-timer, look first for places that don't get the hunting pressure of more accessible country. Also, look for places that few other antelope use. These typically have poorer forage and other resources than more frequented areas. These older bucks are more often than not by themselves.

Stalking mobile harems can be unpredictable. Some years back, not far south of Jeffrey City, Wyoming, I was hunting near a small stink-water marsh. There was only one dirt track within a mile of it, most of the surrounding area had been disrupted by various mining activities, and the bucks wandered about defending their own harems without bothering to try to defend a marked geographic locality. Not far from that marsh, with its green-winged teal and avocet, I'd noticed a place where the grasses were tall and the sagebrush thick. There always seemed to be several antelope harems around, but they'd be tough to approach. I decided to try for a herd bedded down about a mile away.

Unfortunately, they were bedded on the bare, open slope of a low rise, where they could scan the flats thoroughly. The only thing in my favor was that the brush, mostly sage and some rabbitbrush and serviceberry, was pretty tall for the country. Some of it was waist-high, so if I crawled, I'd be hidden. In other places along the route of my planned sneak, however, there was about as much cover as hair on a rattlesnake.

Sneaking through the brush was all right, since I could move along at a crawl. But when I came to shorter vegetation, I had to slither on my belly, and if you have any distance to cover, either method sucks away any vigor you have left. The wind was good, and when I poked my head up and parted the brush carefully, the antelope were still there. To my astonishment, midway in the sneak I frightened another herd of antelope that had been bedded in the sagebrush. They jumped up and raced toward the herd I'd been stalking, which by that time was racing for Montana. As the harem I'd surprised crossed into short brush and spread out, I led the herd buck, who was bringing up the rear, about two lengths and touched off. The bullet kicked up dust behind him, so I lengthened the lead and fired again. The buck put on a burst of speed and streaked through the herd, then veered hard to the right before cartwheeling at least three times to a stop in a cloud of white dust.

Sometimes the country is just too flat and the antelope too spooky to make the traditional, classic antelope sneak worthwhile. If that's the case, try to watch pronghorns from a distance and determine their routines and habits. Then plan your stalk accordingly. Often, in such cases, ambushing is the most productive technique.

On a prairie near a tributary of Wyoming's Sweetwater River, I noticed that several bands of antelope were filing down a shallow ravine to the creek to drink late in the afternoon. I also noticed that they were pretty spooky and would stamp, snort, prance, and toss their heads when they suspected something amiss. Mostly, they were just being skittish, because they knew they were vulnerable going down to water. But this habit was the chink in their armor, and if I could sneak to the downwind side of the trail and wait through the afternoon, I'd be able to get a shot at a buck. I circled downwind and made a loop back to a place I'd previously decided would be the best spot for an ambush "hide." I didn't follow the trail they used because, as spooky as they were, they might head for the border if they scented me anywhere along it. I arranged a few pieces of dead brush and grasses to hide me more completely as I lay in the sagebrush, and waited. Sure enough, toward evening, a band with a decent stud buck trotted nervously toward the water. Again, the shot was anticlimactic. If I'd been seen while approaching the trail or if I'd been scented along it, I'm firmly convinced those skittish antelope wouldn't have followed it to water, and I wouldn't have killed a buck.

Stalking water holes or favored feeding places is pretty similar. And if you're careful, it's a productive way to kill a buck. Much of antelope country can be as dry as the Kalahari and water as scarce as

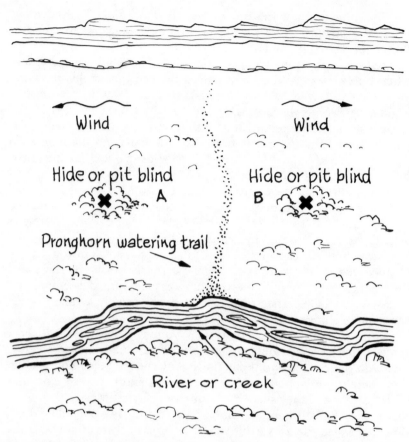

Wind   Wind

Hide or pit blind   Hide or pit blind
    ✖   A   B   ✖

Pronghorn watering trail

River or creek

Pronghorn antelope often use regular trails to and from watering places, and ambushing them along the trails is a good tactic.

two-ounce gold nuggets. As a result, you have the local antelope population pretty well concentrated around water, and ambushing is a good tactic. Use all available cover to sneak up on the ambushing site as if it already contained a trophy buck. Keep track of wind direction. Then conceal yourself, either by constructing a blind or by hiding in a ravine or in brush, and wait. Wind commonly shifts direction, often 180 degrees, after sunup, so plan your ambushing accordingly. While it's true most plains animals don't rely heavily on scent to detect danger, if they get hit with a snootful of man-stink at close range, they'll react.

In places where there is heavy vegetation, ridges, or hills, approaching antelope close enough for a shot is much easier. Staying out of sight isn't such a trick. As with any stalk and sneak, you use what's available, from foot-high sagebrush to thick pine forests, and when there's more cover it's easier to get close. When antelope are in the hills and brush (they'll never be in really thick cover), stalk them as you would deer or elk. Since you're apt to get closer, consideration of hunter noise and wind direction becomes more important. In rolling or thick country, antelope are more prone to depend on hearing and smell to detect danger, since they can't see as far as on the open prairies.

Throughout this chapter, I have maintained that tracking and still

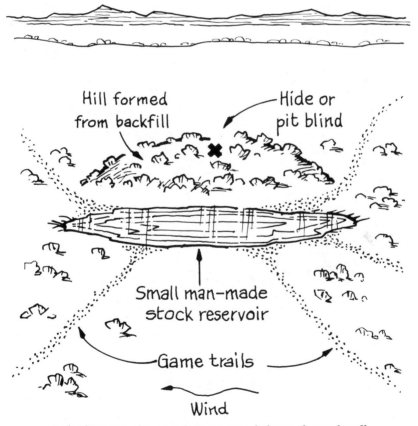

Ambushing pronghorn antelope at a water hole can also work well.

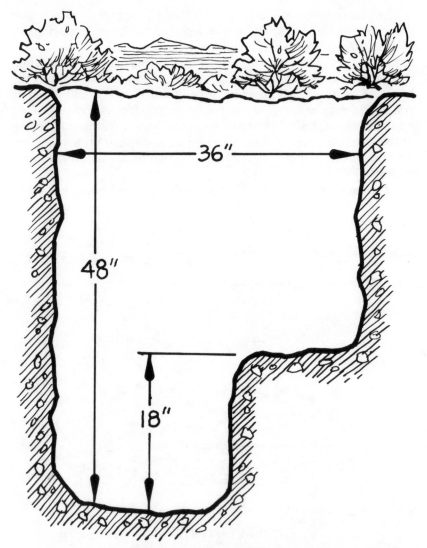

A pit blind dug to ambush pronghorn antelope along a watering trail.

hunting are of less importance on the plain. As with almost any rule in hunting, however, there will be exceptions. One such exception happened on my last antelope hunt, again in the Red Desert. The wind had been blowing for several days, the country was dry and dusty, and the tracks were wiped away as if by an eraser almost as soon as they were made. If you found any tracks at all, they were smoking fresh. Over a low rise was a shallow basin that apparently had some good feed the antelope preferred. Before each time I stalked the basin, I'd check for tracks along its rim. If there were any, I knew that bucks had very recently gone into it and were probably still there feeding. I'd then crouch and crawl to the lip—really only a rise a few feet high—and look in. Antelope were invariably there grazing if I'd seen their tracks first, and on one occasion there was a decent buck at the edge of a herd about two hundred yards away. I settled the cross hairs on his shoulder and pressed the trigger. The .270 barked and punched back into my shoulder, and the buck pitched forward. The sound of the bullet slapping into solid shoulder muscle and bone was whipped away on the prairie wind, but I had a good 15-inch buck.

Before I started this chapter, I tried to remember the longest, most involved stalks I'd pulled off on antelope. One sticks in my mind, and it's a good example of the classic sneak on plains game in general and pronghorn antelope specifically. Early one cold morning on the Red Desert, I found a herd across a vast flat. I knew the buck—I'd located him during the preseason—and he was very big. His jet black horns were heavy and gnarled at the base. They had even, thick prongs and hooked back deeply and wickedly, with two inches of ivory at the tip. I wanted him. Badly. But the damn place was so flat you could see for miles, and there was no tall brush at all. It seemed that the herd wasn't going anyplace where I might sneak up on them, either. There was nothing for it but to try.

I put on my heavy leather jacket and thick wool pants and slithered down the slope into the wind-tortured sagebrush. They were almost a mile away, and the wind was in the right direction. I crawled and crawled. And crawled. The morning became afternoon, my lips cracked, and I'd have given anything for a drink of water. When I raised my head and looked quickly through the binoculars, they were still there, bedded down and spread out through the sagebrush. I crawled on, grateful I'd had the foresight to put on the leather jacket and pants to protect my knees and elbows in the stalk.

Then the antelope were up and grazing again, and I crawled on toward them, noticing they were closer now. I *was* making progress, though for the longest time it hadn't seemed like it. They started feeding off at an angle, and I had to alter the sneak to head them off, but at least the wind was still good and quartering into my face. I was still closing and the herd was still unalarmed. I was licking the dust from my mummified lips, but at last I felt like I'd score. They were nearing shooting range, and the heavy black of the stud buck's horns soared high above his dark face. He was a good one, all right.

As the mellowing sun slid lower toward the mountainous horizon in the west, I found a rest across a badger burrow, put the cross hairs where his neck joined his chest, and so very carefully pressed the trigger. It would be a shame to spoil it here, when I was at last to the easy part. There was the punch of the gun into my shoulder, never felt when you actually shoot at game, the white puff of the bullet slapping into hide, and then the buck jumping forward and collapsing before the sound of the bullet floated back. He was big enough for The Book, if I ever got around to listing him. His horns were just as heavy and massive as I'd thought, measuring 15½ inches. But whether he made The Book or not, whether he was an outstanding trophy or not, I'd value that buck mostly for the sneak it took to get him.

2

Prairie Mule Deer

Mule deer possess perhaps the most formidable combination of senses of any animal on the continent, at least from a hunter's viewpoint. I'm convinced that they, along with moose, have probably the best hearing of any North American game animal—witness the large ears. They have an extraordinary sense of smell. And their eyesight seems as good as that of the pronghorn antelope, most evidenced in open country where they're heavily hunted. Forest game animals sometimes have fairly good eyesight, but most rely on and probably trust it less than do the mule deer. If muleys see something threatening, whether on the plains or in the trees, they'll react and leave the area. This is especially true if they happen to be veterans of several hunting seasons, and most adult bucks are these days, since there are very few places hunters don't get to.

Prairie country typically is flat and has little tall vegetation. The upright hunter is the most obvious thing on the plain, so it's critical to stay out of sight when stalking. Stalk and sneak up on muley bucks just as you would pronghorns; never sell their vision short and try to get away with a sprint across the open to another ravine. If you have to cross within plain sight, either crawl on hands and knees (they may think you're a coyote) or slither on your belly.

The mule deer is also an adaptable animal. Not many years ago the muley was regarded as the whitetail's stupid cousin, because when threatened it would flee for a short distance, then turn around within rifle range to watch the hunter. Though this did sometimes happen (less frequently with older bucks), it was largely because for millennia that strategy had worked for them with everything from wolves to mountain lions to bow-hunting man. With those predators it was a good strategy—the buck would get a safe distance away, then turn to be sure nothing was following. If it was, he'd take off again. But since the appearance of the modern rifle that strategy no longer works, so the mule deer have come up with new ways to cope. No longer do bucks pause and gawk a hundred or so yards up the slope—if they do, they'll never survive to trophy proportions. Foolish bucks are quickly culled from the population, and only the smart and cagey ones survive to pass on their genes. Hence we have a new generation of incredibly wary bucks. And they rely on their magnificent senses, as well. As a result, a trophy mule deer buck these days is arguably the most difficult animal on the continent to take consistently and is therefore one of the most prized.

Trophy bucks are secretive and normally nocturnal during hunting season. They'll run, if they're sure it's safe, when they spot a hunter at a great distance, or they'll hide in timber or brush until they're absolutely certain they've been detected. On the prairie they can detect a hunter at incredible distances, and like the pronghorn antelope and other plains game, they'll flee.

Preseason scouting is one of the best ways to find a good prairie buck. If you do find one, don't alarm him since he's apt to leave the area. Watch from a distance and try to locate favorite bedding areas—you'll probably have to sneak up on one of these when the hunt begins. During hunting season big bucks move about mostly at night and are bedded down in the daytime, usually in difficult-to-approach places. Try to also learn where your buck feeds and waters. It's possible to plan an ambush there or along trails to those places very early or late in the day. If you do decide on an ambush, sneak up to your hiding spot and keep downwind just as you would if you were stalking the animal itself.

Some plains animals, such as pronghorns, don't try to hide when resting or feeding. Not so with mule deer. When they bed down during hunting season, they'll select a place where they're not obvious, such as a gully or a thick patch of sagebrush. It's comparatively easy to locate the tan, white, and black of a resting herd of pronghorns, but it's nearly impossible to spot the neutral colors of a bedded mule deer buck. Bucks rely on their ability to hide, even out on the prairie. If the vegetation is short, you may sometimes find antlers sticking up above it. If you're glassing from a great distance, however, it's tough to tell antler tines from dead sage branches. Watch anything that seems the least bit suspicious. If you find something that seems out of place but you can't tell for certain, glass elsewhere and then come back. The suspicious object may have moved, or the sun may illuminate it from a different direction and make it identifiable. Glassing works best if you know where a buck is living or if you've had enough experience to recognize likely looking cover.

There's a rumor that the biggest mule deer bucks don't come from the prairies and flats. In fact, one major outdoor magazine editor recently stated that they come from the mountains. But I don't agree. I've killed half a dozen bucks that scored around the Boone-and-Crockett minimum, all while hunting on the prairies. And I frightened one of the biggest bucks I've ever seen while pulling off a sneak on a herd of antelope.

That day I'd spent perhaps two hours crawling and slithering through sagebrush and short grass, crouching and groveling up ravines, and generally beating myself up. I was very near the place where I could get a shot, when I crawled into a small depression and came face-to-face with an enormous muley. He was as astounded as I was, and he jumped up and fled across the plain. Not content with frightening me out of five years of life, he ran straight into "my" antelope and they, too, took off. As he raced away, I noticed that his antlers were heavy, with very long points, and they spread at least 7 inches beyond the ear on each side. That would give him a minimum spread of 35 inches! I lusted over that buck for many years.

Back in the midsixties, Wyoming had several late mule deer hunts that lasted until the end of December. One of the better places to collect a prairie buck was in the flat-topped foothills of western Wyoming. Large, sometimes deep, ravines cut through the plain. The north-facing slopes of many of these ravines got less direct exposure from the dessicating summer sun and held more moisture, so stands of aspens and chokecherries grew there. Deer would flock to such places, partly for the feed but also for the cover from the fierce winter squalls. It was almost too easy to sneak up on the lip of one of those big ravines just across from a stand of trees, then frighten a deer up and pot him.

But the big bucks were seldom taken that way. Even in those days, when hunting pressure was light by today's standards and bucks much less wise to the predatory habits of men, you'd seldom find big bucks in the foothills until heavy snows forced them out of the higher country to the west. When they did move in, they'd stay on the flat mesa tops, where they could see anything approaching a mile off. When man or Jeep appeared, they'd take off, and that was the last you'd ever see of them.

One season I hunted just west of Big Piney. A heavy storm had whipped through the night before, plunging the mercury to −30°F and dumping a foot and a half of snow on the flats and probably double that in the high country. Within a day, big tracks began showing up. I spotted one trophy buck I'd have given my first million to collect. Unfortunately, he saw me first, and he headed off in the direction of the Green River. So it went: The best bucks stayed on the flats, and as obvious as I was on the snow, it was impossible to sneak up on them, though I may have had better luck wearing white camo. I never did get a trophy that trip. In the end I settled for a small 4-pointer (10 points by eastern count) from one of those ravines.

Hunting on the prairies generally is better in mid- to late November or early December. Deer rut then; it's usually best around mid-November. During the rut, the younger bucks act as laughable and airheaded as fraternity boys at a house party. While trophy bucks don't become obviously more foolish, they do become slightly more predictable. Where there is a concentration of does, even if there are younger bucks with them, eventually the local stud buck will show up. Then it's up to you to pull off the sneak, if you can outwait them— and that's the tough part. This means staying with a doe group, often for days on end, and watching.

If you're short on time, hunting big bucks during the rut is apt to be frustrating. They move around more visiting various doe groups, and it's tougher to predict their exact whereabouts at a given time. On the prairies, locating a big buck is less than half the battle. The sneak is the most important thing, and pulling it off on a hunter-wise buck requires the patience of Job, the endurance of a decathlete, and a monumental single-mindedness, not to mention the ability to shoot accurately.

Big mule deer bucks are one of the most difficult animals to sneak up on anywhere, but on the open prairies it can be harder than predicting the next eclipse with a handful of chicken bones.

3

Caribou on the Tundra

Like mule deer, caribou occupy a variety of habitat types: low wood-lands in eastern Canada, thick spruce and fir forests in British Columbia, regions well above timberline in the Yukon and Alaska, and vast, featureless tundra barrens north of the Arctic Circle. Hunting caribou in each place requires different tactics, but I am limiting my discussion here to the plains variety.

Though I have hunted caribou in British Columbia, most of those I've hunted come from migratory herds far to the north. Often they leave the high mountains or the coastal plain of the Arctic Ocean during the late summer and drift south. If the weather gets bad, they hurry along, sometimes crossing two major river drainages fifty miles apart in only two days. When the weather is mild, they'll usually stop where they are. They seem to prefer the higher tundra flats between drainages. Some bands migrate more than five hundred miles between early spring and early autumn.

The Gwitch'in Athabascan Indians around Old Crow in the Yukon Territory annually ambush the migration just upriver from their village. Some men kill as many as twenty or thirty animals, then tie the carcasses together and float them downriver. I've witnessed the spectacle several times. They wisely concentrate on killing mature bulls because those are fatter and, as John McPhee once stated, the far north is a fat-starved land. Mature bulls also taste much better before the rut than cows or younger bulls. That's not the case after the rut, however, when mature bulls are nearly inedible. The major harvests occur at Old Crow; Arctic Village, a native "bush" village (accessible only by air or boat) in the Brooks Range; and where the herd crosses the gravel Dempster Highway in the Yukon. Since the Porcupine herd is said to consist of about 175,000 animals, there is probably no serious drain on caribou numbers by hunters. Sport-hunting harvests are negligible. In any case, conservation agencies on both sides of the U.S.–Canada border, which jointly manage the herd, think the caribou are numerous enough to allow a five-animal limit, though natives are allowed substantially more.

Sometime in early or midwinter, the main bands of the Porcupine herd start drifting northward again, many of them trekking up the Porcupine River to near the Arctic Ocean and then west, so that by midspring they are approaching the calving grounds on the Arctic Ocean Plain in the United States' Arctic National Wildlife Refuge (ANWR). Sadly, oil companies and their well-financed lobbies are putting the screw to congressional representatives to open up the ANWR for oil drilling, even though the best estimates indicate that there is less than a few months' worth of fuel located under the plain. The Porcupine caribou herd makes this epic journey yearly, fording swift rivers, climbing high mountain passes, outracing wolves, surviving the harshest winters on the planet, dodging hunters' bullets, losing a liter of blood a week to swarms of ravenous mosquitoes, racing crazily for miles to escape parasitic botflies and warble flies, only to possibly lose the battle for survival because their calving grounds are usurped to provide a few months' heat to the big cities thousands of miles to the south.

A large part of hunting caribou in the Far North and in much of Canada involves catching them as they migrate. Some of this hunting requires no approaching at all. I've shot a number of trophy bulls just waiting at river crossings or mountain passes that I've determined from tracks to be the best places. But I have also located resting bulls on small frost heaves called *pingos*, then spent hours sneaking up on them through tundra composed of lichens, mosses, short grasses, and low brush. More often than not the sneak required crawling and slithering on my belly, which is a pretty universal practice whether in the Arctic or in southern Africa, and just as often the tundra was wet.

If the weather is cold, as it's apt to be in the Far North, it's a miserable way to pull off a sneak.

Caribou, like other game animals that live on the plains, rely on eyesight to detect predators and on running to escape. The same tactics applied to stalking pronghorns or prairie mule deer work with caribou. They seem to pay little attention to what they hear, although odd sounds will alert them. With caribou, to a lesser extent, the same can be said for smell, though this is not true for prairie mule deer and some other species. I've seen big bull caribou hop straight in the air at my sudden scent, run off a hundred yards in a big circle, and come right back into my wind, then do the same thing again. Because of such shenanigans, they've gained the reputation of being pretty foolish.

Caribou have enormous half-moon hooves that splay with their weight and allow them to race across the boggy tundra with relative ease. In a chase, nothing can catch them. Until relatively recently, their only real predators have been wolves. Because the wolves stood no chance of catching them in a straight chase, caribou weren't especially alarmed by what they saw as long as they could identify it and keep an eye on it. I've seen caribou approach several wolves to within forty or fifty yards. Then they'd trot and prance off as if they'd frightened themselves, circle, and approach the wolves again. They may possibly have developed this behavior to confuse wolves, which typically hunt caribou by driving them to an ambush. If caribou act unpredictably, wolves would have a tougher time driving them to the spot where other pack members are lying in ambush. Hunters with long-range rifles see such things and brand the caribou as dumb.

On the other hand, if caribou have been hunted and shot at by man before or have recently had a very close scrape with wolves, they can be quite skittish. I can recall at least half a dozen times when bulls raced off because they'd glimpsed me briefly hundreds of yards away. I don't normally expect them to hang around and act foolish when I'm hunting them, though sometimes they do.

For many years I spent about eight weeks in the Arctic wilderness hunting, photographing, climbing mountains, and running rivers, until I float out to some small native village sometimes more than three hundred miles away or rendezvous with a bush plane on a tiny river bar. On these expeditions, I'm often more than four hundred miles from the nearest pavement, hospital, or grocery store. It's impossible for me to carry enough food to live on for this length of time, so I'm forced to survive in part off the land. Hunting takes on added meaning when you must do it in order to eat. I usually have a plentiful supply of meat: There are moose, ptarmigan, grayling, waterfowl, and caribou. But once in a while I run out of meat, and more than once stalking a caribou bull has been important for more than antlers. On such sneaks, I act on the assumption that the bull is as skittish as an old Wyoming pronghorn, and I take special pains to stay out of sight.

One season a few years back, Cheri Flory and I had been out of meat for a week. We'd earlier killed a nice Dall ram in the mountains seventy miles upriver, but what we hadn't eaten had been appropriated by a cantakerous grizzly that had no respect for humans or their guns. The bear had wandered into camp one evening, pulled what was left of the meat out of a tree, and wandered off with it, presumably for a snack. I don't mind eating fish, but Cheri does; and besides, the grayling we'd caught did not quite supply enough energy for living in the bush. We were both yearning for red meat. At this point we weren't picky, so any legal game would do. We floated down the swift, surging river, pausing to glass from the bluffs.

About midday we saw a flash on a vast tundra plain more than two miles away. Then we spotted more white specks. They turned out to be the silver necks of bull caribou, which seemed to be grazing slowly east. We slid down the bluff and paddled the inflatable raft across the river. Then, while Cheri set up camp, I stalked off after the bulls.

The first half mile was easy, though wet. I stalked through a muskeg bog, most of the time up to my knees in water and muck. The dwarf Arctic birch was taller than I was, so I could stand and make fairly good time in spite of the muck. Once out of the bog, though, I had to crouch and move across the spongy tundra on a line that would head off the grazing bulls. Walking on tundra where you sink more than six inches at every step is tiring, and doing it while crouched is exhausting. Stopping for rests and moving only when the bulls were occupied with feeding, it took me several hours to cover the next mile.

By that time the bulls were on a low tundra rise and could look down on me and my stalking route, so I had to crawl on hands and knees through the tundra puddles. Except for the puddles and tundra and lowbush blueberries, it was virtually the same stalk I'd made on pronghorn antelope a dozen times. I must have stalked for two more hours like this, though it seemed much longer. Eventually the bulls bedded on the point of the rise and could see everything on the plain for miles. Now I was slithering on my belly, thoroughly soaked, exhausted, cold, and miserable, and wishing I were home watching a football game and feasting on pizza and beer.

I was about three hundred yards away when one bull stood and stared hard in my direction. I lay motionless for what seemed an entire month, hoping he'd forget about me. No such luck. After considerable time, he whirled and sprinted in the caribou's odd, ground-eating gait in the direction of the Yukon. The others hopped up as one and followed without as much as a glance in my direction. I was as dejected as I had ever been, partly because I'd failed and was soaked and cold, but even more because I knew how Cheri would feel.

I sloshed back across the wet tundra for camp, feeling a hopeless failure when, luck of luck, I noticed caribou antlers above some bare, low willow branches a quarter mile away. I dropped to my belly again—I was taking no chances—and crawled toward the bull with renewed vigor. Somehow, I knew I'd get that bull if I was careful. And I was. The wind was quartering into my face, and it probably took me more than an hour to close on him. In the end, I was only forty yards away. His prehistoric-looking antlers floated above the short brush, and he wasn't in the least suspicious. I stood up slowly and flicked off the safety, then whistled. The bull jumped up and stared. One bullet broke his shoulder, angled into the heart, and killed him instantly. Though I shot him for the meat, he was a trophy bull with big, double shovels, a 56-inch beam, and a 44-inch spread. I quickly boned out the hindquarters and backstraps, tied them to the pack frame, and trotted off to camp. We polished off one entire backstrap that night—it's amazing what living in the Arctic wilds can do to your appetite! In the morning we returned for the forequarters, but a grizzly had seized the carcass and I had no wish to dispute it with him.

When caribou are on a feeding binge, they can be oblivious to whatever else is going on around them. This is particularly true if the brush is two or three feet tall; then their line of vision is below the brush, and if they're feeding frantically, as they sometimes do when they find a concentration of good browse during the migration, it's possible to walk right into their midst. A herd of browsing caribou makes quite a bit of noise, crunching fallen leaves, breaking branches, grunting, bellies rumbling. Then you can not only pay less attention to staying out of sight but also disregard noise somewhat and stalk more quickly.

Once, when my hunting buddy Rick Lovell and I were floating down a northern river, we spotted a band of twenty caribou bulls grazing in dwarf willows along the river. They were on top of a ten-foot bluff, and we took advantage of this to float close to the bulls. If any of them noticed us as we approached, they didn't show it. Even if they had seen us floating up on them, they may not have run, since most game seems to view floating hunters as debris or perhaps swimming animals until the hunters get close enough to be recognized or scented.

When we reached the bluff, we stepped out and tied the raft below the bulls' line of vision. Their great antlers bobbed about in the low brush. They were feeding frantically before starting the next spurt of their migration. They were so busy feeding that their eyes were mostly below the tops of the dwarf willows. We walked hurriedly toward the bulls, closing quickly.

By the time we'd gotten within eighty yards, most of the bulls were still feeding, though one or two were staring. Rick had picked the one he wanted and was resting the rifle across my shoulder. At the blast of the 7mm Magnum, the bull hunched slightly, took several steps, and collapsed. The caribou were still unalarmed, though most were staring, and they didn't run until we approached Rick's bull. It was a good one with long upper points, some upper palmation, and a nice spread.

We had made too much noise on that stalk, partly because we were breaking our way through dried tangles of dwarf willows and partly because the fallen leaves were as noisy as Cheetos underfoot, but the bulls had paid no attention because they were making precisely the same sounds. The wind was blowing from us out over the river, so they couldn't catch our scent, and the first bulls to see us were younger and less experienced ones that probably thought we were other caribou. Herd animals make noises when they feed, so being silent is less critical when stalking them. Foreign noises, such as metal against metal, the squeak of a sling swivel, or the scraping of brush against stiff fabrics, will quickly alert game, though.

There's little doubt that, on the whole, caribou on the tundra plains of the far north are much easier to stalk than pronghorn antelope, mule deer on the prairies, or most African plains species. Some of them, however, are just as skittish as the wisest Red Desert pronghorn, so it's best to stay out of sight when sneaking up on a trophy barren-ground caribou. I've been burned often enough that I *never* take it for granted that it will be an easy stalk.

4

African Plains Game

In Africa today the term *plains game* more often than not refers to all game except the big five (leopard, lion, buffalo, elephant, and rhino) — in other words, everything but dangerous game. In this chapter, however, I'm using it to refer to big game that spends at least part of its time on the plains.

The gemsbok (an oryx) is typically found in brushy and open savannas, as in the Kalahari Desert and many other places in southern Africa. It relies mostly on vision to detect danger and on running to escape it. I once hunted them in some large, dry pans in Namibia. (Pans are lake beds that are typically dry, sometimes for years on end.) There was very little cover there that we could use on a stalk. The gemsbok had been shot at by both native hunters and sportsmen and had apparently been chased by several lion prides that roamed the area, so they were very spooky. They'd move off if you got within eight hundred or so yards, and they'd trot off quickly if you somehow managed to get closer than that.

Gemsbok aren't normally difficult to get, so we'd allowed only two days to collect one plus a hartebeest before leaving to hunt buffalo and kudu, the prizes of this trip. We tried following the gemsbok, but there wasn't enough cover to enable us to get within a quarter mile. We tried crouching and scurrying, hoping we'd look like some small, queer grazers. We tried stalking out onto the pan before first light. We even dug pits and tried to drive the big, colorful antelope past them. In a brief moment of frustration, we tried chasing them in the Land Rover, but the terrain was too rough for us to catch up with them. Nothing worked.

There was only one thing left to try, and that was to slither across the barren flats like I used to after Wyoming pronghorn. We could see the big, donkey-shaped gemsbok with their skewer-sharp, back-slanting horns silhouetted against the dawn sky. I slid out of the Land Rover and lay on my belly as it drove off. Dust hung in the still air a mile away long after the Rover had gone. I started crawling toward the gemsbok, which seemed deceptively near. What little wind there was was good, and it quartered into my face. I'd brought a jug of water and a bit of biltong in my daypack, so I was set for the day.

I crawled out across the bare, white-dust pan, the gemsbok filing toward some small, two- to three-foot rises in the direction I was heading. I crawled on as the sun climbed steadily higher. It was June, which is comparable to December in the Northern Hemisphere, and very fortunately on the desert, it was one of the coolest months of the year. Even so, by midday it was too warm. I crawled on, glad for the water and the biltong, toward the rises and the gemsbok. The animals just seemed to be standing; they hadn't noticed me, or if they had they weren't paying much attention. The wind was steady and favorable. The sun passed its zenith, then slowly began its descent to the northwest and the South Atlantic. On I crawled.

Once I found the broken skull and bones of a baboon that had apparently been caught trying to cross the pans by some predator, probably a lion. The find made me look around carefully. It seemed to be an omen, because hours later I saw a thin plume of dust, then something lean racing at me, and then another of whatever it was. They turned out to be cheetahs that had thought I was something good to eat. For my own safety, I stood up and shouted them off. That, of course, spooked off the gemsbok, which had still been bedded. If it hadn't been for this, I think that belly-slithering tactic would have worked, because the gemsbok had been paying absolutely no attention to me, and I had gotten within about six hundred yards. But that was the end of it.

Red lechwe, the most common of the lechwe, are antelope of the marshes, within which they spend their time on open, soggy plains. I hunted red lechwe in the Okavango Delta of northern Botswana. Here water flows in slowly from Angola and places north. The delta is composed of vast, thousand-acre islands. When I hunted there in 1989, much of it was wilderness and there were elephants, giraffes, lions, leopards, hyenas, buffalo, hippos, lechwe, warthogs, bushbuck, waterbuck, reedbuck, kudu, sitatunga, and crocodiles on the islands, in the marshes, and in the rivers, sometimes in astonishing numbers.

The lechwe kept to vast, water-covered, grassy plains, where the water was from ankle- to knee-deep. They were often in herds of two or three hundred, and if there was an island of palms or a thicket of acacia in the marsh, we could sometimes get within rifle range. More often than not, though, we had to stalk them in the open across the low grasses while sloshing through clear Okavango water. The lechwe paid little attention when we were seven hundred yards away, but they began to take notice if we got within four hundred and became pretty spooky if we got closer than that. In places, they were practically unhunted by man. I'm sure the many lions, leopards, and hyenas took them, however, so it was their nature to keep distance between them and anything suspicious. If we got too close, they'd simply walk away.

There were eight of us hunting that day—professional hunter Willie Phillips, Cheri, the Bayei and Bushman trackers, and me—so we were more than a little obvious as we sloshed across the marshy plains. The lechwe got very nervous if we fanned out, but if we approached in single file we could get closer. Even so, it was tough to get close to larger herds; since they were spread out, they could see our file from an angle as we splashed across the flats. We had better luck with smaller groups, because they were looking at us head-on as we approached in single file, and we thus gave the appearance of being only one beast. The best males, however, were invariably in the large, hard-to-approach herds.

We sneaked up on several herds, but they always took off before we got close enough for a sure shot. There was no brush or termite mound to use as a rifle rest, and if we would sit down in the water and grass to make the shot, we couldn't see the lechwe, so it was necessary to use a wobbly forked stick to shoot from. With this, unless we were fairly close, there was too much chance of wounding, so we had to get closer than we might have under better circumstances. Another problem was that a good buck would quickly lose himself in the herd.

We hunted one frustrating day without luck, then returned to camp by *mokorro*, a dugout canoe. Camp was pitched on an island beside the idyllic, diamond-clear Vumbora River. As the lithe, muscular Bayei poled back through the papyrus swamps to the river and thence to camp, I couldn't help but feel very good, even though we'd had no luck hunting. I was in the land of my boyhood fantasies, and it was every bit as good as those idealized visions. In fact, I was surprised a piece of pristine Africa still existed, and even without the hunting, this expedition into the heart of the Okavango would be something I'd remember fondly all my life. As we glided along the river in the dusk, hippos grunted nearby on either side, a pride of lions suddenly began roaring only four or five hundred yards away, and thousands of frogs croaked and whistled. The Southern Cross hung next to a crescent moon in a star-thick sky, and I was as happy as it's possible to be.

We were back on the Vumbora early in the morning, the Bayei poling us back through the papyrus, with large beasts crashing through the fifteen-foot reeds, to the wet lechwe plains. It was obvious the lechwe didn't need to rely on hearing or scent to detect predators. There were so many other animals wandering through the Okavango making all sorts of noises that they really couldn't rely much on hearing for safety. And they could see danger on the marshy flats long before they'd ever smell it. Short of using a snorkel, I couldn't figure out how to get close.

Willie decided on a trick that had worked for me before on mountain sheep. Apparently, animals can't count, or at least are perplexed by a group of people that suddenly becomes two groups. Willie, Cheri, and company stopped on the open plain, and Joseph, the head Bayei tracker and hunter, and I circled. The lechwe watched us and then Willie's group, which was larger and more obvious and was milling about purposely to keep the lechwe's attention. Occasionally the lechwe in the small herd would look at us, but they were much more fascinated by Willie's group. Joseph and I were closing, and most of the herd had all but forgotten about us as they watched Willie's band walking in circles, squatting, and doing odd things. We were in the open, painfully obvious with nothing to hide us, but the herd, including the big male, was totally absorbed by the other group's antics.

We were at last getting close, and luck finally went our way. There was a small, dead acacia with a branch at just the right height. I rested the .270 on the branch, held low on the shoulder of the bull as he stood quartering to me, and carefully pressed the trigger. I heard the bullet hit, and the big bull bolted into some high grass. Joseph jammed his thumb low into his shoulder and twisted it to show me where the animal had been hit. It took eight of us circling in the high grass and knee-deep water a half hour to find the trophy lechwe, stone dead. The bullet had hit just where I'd aimed and had taken out the heart and lungs. His unusually heavy horns measured a bit over 26 inches—quite good for the Okavango.

Part II
Forest and Savanna Game

It can be argued that there are no true forest animals among North America's game species. The white-tailed deer that may seem to inhabit almost exclusively the forests of the Northeast or Canada actually seeks out old burns, abandoned farms, and other openings in the woods to find the shrubs and browse that grow in such places. The black-tailed deer, usually an animal of the thick, wet forests of coastal Alaska south to the Northwest, comes to open beaches to feed on kelp and lick salt from the rocks, seeks out old burns or clearcuts, and is even found above timberline. The black bear, another species that typically inhabits thick North American forests, also looks for openings—tundra plains thick with lowbush blueberries, Montana or Idaho huckleberry and gooseberry thickets, and the sometimes open salmon streams of coastal British Columbia. So when I speak of forest game here, I refer to animals that at times and in certain places spend a great deal of time in the woods.

Forest animals rely less on eyesight to detect danger than do plains animals, since a predator will be too close by the time they see it. They rely more heavily, instead, on hearing and scent and can often sneak off before the hunter or predator is even aware of their presence. Some animals—mule deer, for instance—rely more on eyesight on the plains or open above-timberline basins and more on hearing and scent in forests.

In forests, hunters generally still-hunt rather than spot to locate game and then sneak to close on it. Still hunting consists of moving slowly and quietly, into the wind if possible, trying to find what's there before it senses you and flees. It's an exciting way to hunt, especially if you're reasonably sure there's game in the vicinity.

Tracking is used less commonly, mostly because it's more difficult, but it can be every bit as effective. Tracking is following the prints made by your quarry as it moves over soft ground or snow. The goal isn't always to follow the trail blindly to its end; as often as not, if you do that, the quarry will sense you and move away before you're aware of it. Instead, tracking should be following the trail to determine what the animal is doing, and then adjusting your stalking to that. For

Ace Zimbabwe professional hunter Russell Tarr with my big waterbuck. The water-buck is a typical forest and savanna species.

example, if a big mule deer buck has begun to meander but isn't showing signs of feeding (cropped twigs or forbs pulled out of the ground), it's looking for a bed. Since many game animals, big muleys especially, bed downwind and within sight of their backtrails, following the tracks blindly will only play into the trophy buck's plan. He'll see or smell you and take off. Instead, you have to anticipate the buck and make loops downwind of his trail or, in some instances, move along parallel and downwind of the trail and surprise him.

A savanna is defined by author Raymond Dasmann as a place where trees "grow either singly or in groves" in a grassland. Dasmann wrote *Wildlife Biology*, a textbook I used as a graduate student in the seventies. That definition is as good as any, so I'll use it here.

Savanna hunting can often be similar to forest hunting because savanna animals generally hole up in the scattered woods that break up the grass- or brushlands. This is true with elk, mule deer, whitetails, moose, and kudu, among others, and when hunting them in these pockets of woods, you may want to use forest hunting tactics.

5

Muleys in Timber

Mule deer live in about every type of habitat found in North America: open plains, thick forests, savannas, deserts so dry in Sonora and southern Arizona that few ungulates can survive there, high above-timberline basins, even marshy forests in central British Columbia. It's difficult to decide exactly where mule deer are found most commonly, but in the classic muley states of Colorado, Wyoming, and Montana, they're often found in mountainous savanna country. They're found less frequently in thickly forested places, but with the heavy hunting pressure they usually get these days, they are spending more and more of their time in the woods. In places where there are forests and where deer are hunted, most trophy bucks spend their daylight hours in the trees, and those that do this can be tough to collect.

Mule deer begin rutting about the middle of November and, on most of their range, have pretty well run out of steam by the end of the first week of December (they breed about a month later on the Sonora Desert). If you have the opportunity to hunt during the rut, still-hunt and watch around bands of does. Eventually, the local stud buck will show up there. If you don't have much time, stalking during the rut is apt to be frustrating, since big bucks are constantly on the move checking various doe herds and are hard to pinpoint at any given time. Contrary to poplar hunter myth, big bucks do not become more foolish during the rut; only subadult bucks do.

In the October 1988 issue of *Outdoor Life*, I wrote about a basic behavioral change I'd noticed in old mule deer bucks since I started hunting them in the early sixties. Back then, when hunting pressure was lighter, it seemed that the bucks, even the big ones, ran from danger as soon as they detected it. Today, however, most trophy bucks stay hidden until they're absolutely certain they've been detected. With the armies of redshirts afield these days, they've learned that to run means to get shot at and that if they lie absolutely still in timber or brush, 99 percent of the hunters won't see them. They've shifted, then, from being primarily runners to hiders, thus becoming a bit like the whitetail. This behavioral change places new emphasis on finesse in stalking, and patience becomes even more important. If you hurry along, you won't even see a trophy buck, let alone shoot one.

Hunting mule deer in forests (as opposed to more open savanna country, which I will discuss later) is often a tense, exciting game. Most hunters who actually do go into thick timber after a trophy buck—and there are surprisingly few—still-hunt.

When you still-hunt mule deer in timber, move slowly and carefully (*carefully* takes on added meaning when after trophy bucks in thick trees, since you'll be very close when and if you see one). Take a step or two, stop, and look around. Look into the shadows for something that doesn't quite belong, such as a leg, a light-colored rump, or an antler tine. Listen carefully and suspect every sound, even though it'll probably only be a red squirrel or a chickadee searching the tree bark for ants' eggs. If you hurry, you'll never get a buck in the timber. Mule deer have extraordinary hearing—the best of any animal I've hunted—so wear "quiet" clothing, such as wool and soft-soled boots, sneakers, or moccasins. Concentrate on walking and sneaking silently. If you have to slow to a turtle's crawl to be silent, do it. Still-hunt into the wind, because a muley's smell is nearly as good as its hearing.

In my early years of mule deer hunting, I'd usually still-hunt the more open slopes of Utah's Wasatch Mountains. I'd hunt mostly early and late in the day, up the brushy, thick north- or east-facing slopes, trying to scare a buck out of the trees below and onto the opposite, open west- or south-facing slope where I could get a shot. Back in the sixties, this worked. But as more hunters came to the hills, the deer that showed themselves during the day got shot off, and the only good bucks to survive were those that took to the timber during shooting hours.

The first time I stalked into the timber after a big buck, I made all the mistakes. I'd seen the buck at the edge of timber in the last few minutes of shadowy light, and as I watched his big antlers in the dusk, I made up my mind to go in after him in the morning. I returned at first light and stalked along through the snow. I was wearing jeans, typical western hunting garb, and before long they were frozen solid to knee height. The cuffs scraped together noisily as I still-hunted along. At that point in my hunting career, I'd mostly been potting deer in the open two or three hundred yards across canyons, and I hadn't yet realized how keen their senses were.

My rifle hung from my shoulder just as it always had, my hands were plunged deep in my pockets, and I moved along at a fairly steady clip since the tracks were obvious in the new snow. I came to a ravine and forced my way through the creek willows as branches scraped noisily against my frozen jeans. I saw the buck through a corridor in the trees as he jumped to his feet, cleared a deadfall in one

A good mule deer bagged in a mountainous forest in Utah.

Well-used deer trail between feeding areas on an open slope to forest bedding cover.

bound, and disappeared. I didn't even have time to get my hands out of my pockets, let alone free the rifle, bring it up, and shoot.

Within a few years I'd learned the importance of still hunting into the wind, wearing quiet clothing such as wool or flannel, stalking in soft-soled footgear or even stocking feet, and keeping the gun ready and my thumb near the safety while staying aware and watching carefully ahead. Eventually I got good at stalking muleys in timber. Not only did I become more successful, but I learned a new and more exciting way to hunt. And I found where the trophy bucks were hiding.

Not too many seasons ago, I found a trophy buck's hiding spot. I'd been in the area hunting blue grouse before deer season and had found the "center area," (or "core area," but since this term has been used to define several different concepts, I'll use "center area" here) of the buck's home range in a big stand of Douglas fir, spruce, and aspen. Several game trails led through the stand. There was a marshy seep in a thicket of willows on the slope, and above that, a thick tangle of willows and aspen saplings where the buck bedded. The bark on half a dozen big saplings had been rubbed away when the buck had polished his antlers. Sixty-five yards from the bedding area was an open slope where manzanita, chokecherries, bitterbrush, grasses, and forbs grew. That buck had everything he needed to wax fat and healthy within a radius of two hundred yards.

First I found his huge tracks (they were four inches long!), and then one evening I saw him. His antlers spread at least 30 inches and had long points. I hunted him hard through the better part of the following week. I hadn't seen him again, though, but I knew he was still around; his big, fresh tracks were everywhere on the trails in the timber and on the open slope where he fed, apparently at night. Waiting wasn't going to work—the big buck was too smart to show himself in the open during deer season—so I would have to go in after him.

I moved slowly into the timber along one of the trails, stalking carefully into the wind, watching everything ahead and to the sides, listening, and even smelling (mule deer, as well as other members of the deer family, Cervidae, can have a strong, musky, pungent, though not always unpleasant, odor). I knew where he probably was—in the center area in the midst of that thick aspen tangle—but sneaking in there, let alone seeing him in time to get a shot, was the trick. I found a trail that let me approach upwind, and I eased along it. I moved so slowly that I could have fallen asleep. I mostly crawled on hands and knees to avoid intertwined branches above the trail, and I pushed the gun along in front of me. If I stayed on hands and knees, I could move quietly on the well-trod loam.

I was beginning to feel pretty good about the sneak. If he was there, maybe I *would* get a shot after all. When I had started into the tangle, I had figured my chances were slim. I'd crawl a foot or two, stop, then scan everything carefully. In that tangle, I knew I wouldn't be able to see the whole animal or even any very large part of him. I'd have to find something small—an eye, a nostril, or the flick of an ear—before he became aware of what was happening. Then I'd need to find a place where I could get a bullet through the branches and to slap the trigger quickly before the buck could jump, or I'd have no chance at him.

And that was just how it worked out. I saw some antler tines that I had at first thought were branches—until they moved. Then an ear flicked at a fly, and I could tell which way he was facing. I sat up, scooted a few inches to my right to see around a deadfall, and found the place where his neck joined his head. I eased the rifle up very slowly, afraid the buck would sense the movement, then scrunched down to shoot under a twig. When I did so, the buck's neck was hidden from view behind some grass. But I knew where it was from the ears and eye, so I squeezed off. The muzzle blast shattered the thick silence. I bulled my way toward where I'd seen him, unsure whether I'd killed him. He was there, fourteen paces away. The bullet had broken his neck as he lay chewing his cud, and the antlers were very good, spreading almost 30 inches. In the end, trophies fade into the wall, but you remember stalks like that one.

In timber, tracking can work even better than still hunting, though unfortunately it's an art that isn't practiced much these days. In Africa the tracking, or spooring, prowess of native groups such as the Bushman of the Kalahari, the Bayei of the Okavango, and the Matabele of Zimbabwe is so incredible that you might swear it was witchcraft. But I haven't met anyone in North America in twenty years who was even a little adept at tracking, let alone specialized in tracking one species, such as mule deer.

I suppose no one practices tracking anymore because it's just too hard. In a generation that lives vicariously through TV sitcoms and soaps and is too lazy to get up and turn the channel without remote control, I suppose it's expecting too much that hunters put in the time and effort needed to learn tracking. Tracking requires not only a great deal of concentration but also enough self-discipline to make yourself go even slower when you're already traveling at less than a yard per minute, an understanding of your own capabilities and shortcomings as well as animal behavior, and a lot of time and work. It's not something you can pick up from a sixty-minute video. The only way to become good at it is to practice.

When a mule deer walks, the hind feet are placed exactly in the print left by the forehooves. The forehoof of a good adult buck measures 3½ to 4 inches long. The walking stride of a big mule deer buck is between twenty-three and twenty-six inches. If a buck's trail meanders among plants and there are nipped shoots or cropped twigs, that buck was feeding. If the track is meandering but there are no signs of browsing, the buck is looking for a place to bed.

The trotting stride is used almost as often as walking. When a mature buck trots, the hoofprints will appear individually and measure from thirty-three to forty inches apart, depending on terrain, speed, and the animal's size. When a buck is frightened, it often gallops. The right forehoof strikes the ground first, and the left forehoof hits a short distance in front of that spot. As the hind legs come forward, the right hind hoof contacts the ground first, followed by the left. When you're looking at a galloping track, the forehoof prints are behind the hind ones, and the left tracks are a bit ahead of the right. The gallop is an energy-consuming stride, and a buck won't keep it up for long. Usually he'll revert back to a trot as soon as he feels safe. When he's secure in timber or brush, he'll stop to watch and listen at his backtrail.

When a mule deer buck bounds (often incorrectly called the stot), he's *very* scared. Bounding consumes more energy than any other stride, and a buck will only use it for short periods of time. The bounding strides of nine adult bucks I've measured ranged from twenty-two to twenty-nine feet, depending on the size of the animal, the terrain, and how badly he was frightened. Bounding may appear awkward, but it's an effective stride for getting over rough country in a hurry.

Again, the best way to recognize tracks is to get field experience. Watch for deer during the summer or late winter when they're less wary. Look at a yearling buck's track. How does it compare with those of the doe and fawn you trailed last week or the big buck the week before that?

Determining a track's age can be a tricky business—the most difficult part of tracking. To become good at it you need to practice. The best way to do so is to make tracks of your own in various soil types and under different conditions common to the area you'll be hunting.

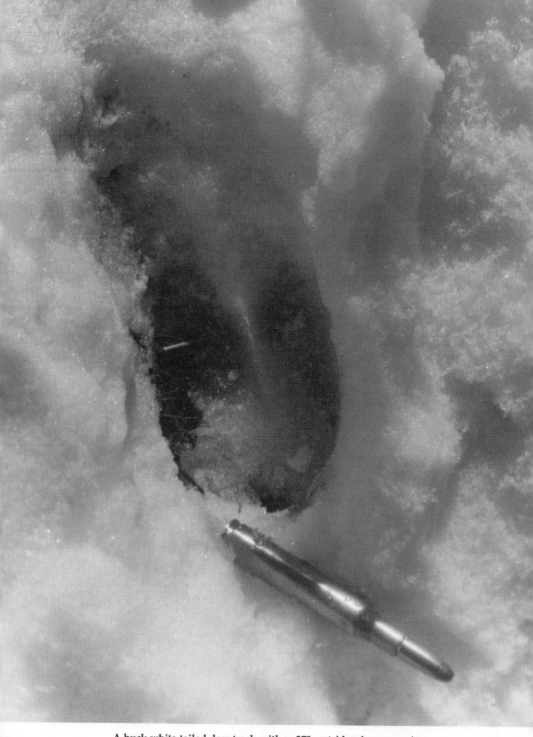

A buck white-tailed deer track with a .270 cartridge for comparison.

Note how they change in two, eight, ten, and twenty-four hours. When hunting, I often carried a belt knife with a handle made from a deer's foot. For years I would press that hoof into different soil types around camp and make mental note of the changes over time. Along with field experience, that little exercise taught me more about how to

This is the loop method of tracking, and it works for tracking any game in timber or brush, not just mule deer.

Mule deer, as well as most members of the deer family, hide in timber during the day and feed on open slopes in the evening, night, and morning. In the West, where it is often quite dry, the north- and east-facing slopes are the only timbered slopes.

age tracks than everything I've read and heard combined. Humidity, weather, temperature, soil type, and other factors must be considered when aging tracks, and only practice can teach you to do it right.

If you're tracking a big mule buck, be aware that he typically will pause just inside of timber or brush to watch his backtrail (these days he'll seldom do it in the open, where he might get shot). In timber, when you're stalking any trophy animal that's been hunted—and this applies especially to deer—nine times out of ten he'll buttonhook on his backtrail to be downwind of following danger. So you should either make loops on the downwind side of the trail, returning to it once in a while for confirmation, or stalk parallel to and downwind of the track. The second method works better if you're more sure where the animal is going or if you can see the trail, for example downslope in snow.

I once flushed a buck while still-hunting through a heavy stand of timber. The buck took off, and I sat on a blowdown to let him settle down a bit before taking up the trail. I was aware that he'd watch his backtrail from the trees somewhere on ahead. If I showed up again, he'd take off even more frightened. But if I didn't, he'd slow down and eventually bed again, though he would remain alert to anything following him.

I waited about an hour before I took up the trail, and I read from the tracks what had happened. At first the buck had bounded through the trees, then he had stopped to watch his backtrail on the other side of an opening created by a windstorm years earlier. When nothing had showed on his backtrail, he had trotted off, considerably less frightened. The trail crossed a ravine in the timber, and he had then paused on the other side to once again watch his backtrail. When I didn't show, he had trotted on awhile, then slowed to a walk—he was calming down. I still didn't show up, so the buck walked on, calm now, and within a quarter mile his trail started to meander as he looked for a bed. It took me all day to get to the point where his trail started meandering, and by that time he was over his fright. Mule deer in general are not nervous, flighty animals like whitetails; they're calm, calculating, and cool.

I knew he was bedded not far ahead and probably had made a buttonhook on the downwind side of his trail so that he'd be able to scent and probably see any approaching danger. I took my boots off and stuffed them into the daypack, did the same with the rifle sling, then walked twenty-five yards above and downwind of the trail. I made loops downwind of the trail, occasionally returning to the track

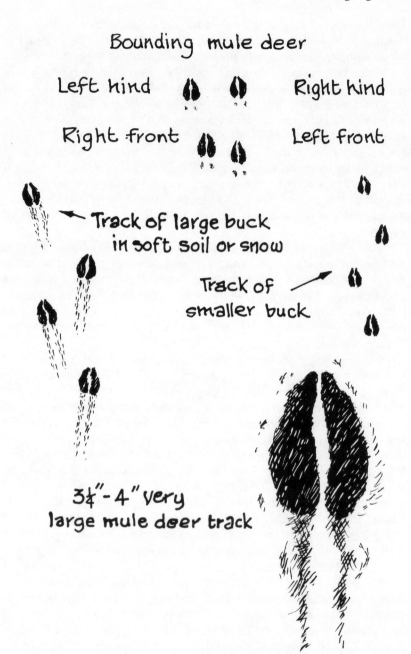

Bounding mule deer

Left hind   Right hind

Right front   Left front

← Track of large buck
in soft soil or snow

Track of →
smaller buck

3¼"-4" very
large mule deer track

Mule deer tracks and strides.

for confirmation that I was still stalking in the right direction. Although I hadn't seen the buck and didn't know where he was, I did feel pretty sure he'd be downwind of the trail, so I sneaked along, pausing often to look and listen. Then, late in the afternoon, I saw something that didn't quite belong. It seemed to be a large, dark knothole on a light, weathered deadfall. I looked at it for eons. Then it blinked! The buck was up and over the deadfall as I whipped the .270 to my shoulder and slapped the trigger, almost as though I were shooting grouse. The buck disappeared and a pinch of hair floated slowly down in the still air. He was a good one, too, but again, I valued him more for the stalk than for the trophy.

Of all the hunting I do, I prefer tracking in timber. It's the most adrenaline pumping, it requires every bit of concentration you can muster, it demands an understanding of game behavior, and it often calls for very quick shooting. I love it because of the demands it puts on me as a hunter. It's a tense, exciting game.

Hunting mule deer in more open savanna country is a slightly different proposition. Actually, stalking in some savannas falls somewhere between doing so in timber and on the plains. Normally there are openings between stands of brush or trees. Mule deer bucks bed and hide in the trees during the day and feed in the openings at night. Most mule deer country is of the savanna type and usually is also mountainous. Over the years I've developed a method of stalking mule deer in these parts. I call it "canyon hunting."

There are basically three strategies for combing a canyon for mule deer. The first is to push, or start, deer into a place where you can get a shot. You want to drive the buck from the timber on the north- or east-facing slope and out onto the opposite, more open slope. Since mule deer have incredibly keen senses and are apt to discover you and move away before you're ready for them to do so, you have to stalk and sneak up on any place that seems suspicious. Move quietly and slowly into the timber. If you burst through the brush like the defensive line of the Chicago Bears, you'll frighten bucks into an all-out run well up the canyon. It's wise not to panic a buck into an all-out run because often the opposite slope is three hundred or more yards away, and potting a buck that's bounding and dodging through brush, ravines, and rocks at that range is difficult. Move in easily, and let the bucks sneak off at their own pace. When still-hunting and stalking through timber or brush, keep aware of any openings—remember, you have to shoot out of the brush across the canyon to the opposite slope.

Sometimes stands of brush are small and the retreat route predictable enough that you can get a big buck moving onto the opposite slope by simply letting your scent drift to him. Early in the morning and after sunset, the air is cold and dense and in most places drifts downhill; get above a buck's cover at these times. During daylight hours, the air heats and becomes less dense and flows uphill. Then, get below the timber and watch the ravine or canyon heads and ridges above the trees. It usually takes awhile for a buck to react from scent alone, and even more so if he's reasonably sure he hasn't been detected.

With a very small patch of cover, you can throw rocks in order to flush a deer. Once, in Nevada's Ruby Mountains, I tossed rocks into a thick tangle of willows about the size of a large living room. The willows were on a completely open slope on a high ridge, and there was no other vegetation capable of hiding anything larger than a jackrabbit. I just had a hunch about it. I tossed one rock, waited, tossed others, waited more, then sat down to enjoy the view. Idly I tossed one more rock, figuring that by that time no deer was in the patch of brush. But I heard a peculiar *thunk*, and the next moment a huge buck crashed out of the willows as if the hounds of hell were after him. I was so rattled that my first two shots missed clean. I'm not sure whether I settled down or was just lucky, but the third one caught him in the back of the neck just as he was disappearing over the opposite ridge.

Mule deer are surprisingly cool under pressure, and more than once I've watched them outwait deer hunters very nearby. I'm sure they've outwaited me. In fact I know that more than once they *almost* outwaited me, because I've discovered deer at times when I decided to walk through a suspicious patch of brush after letting my scent drift into it didn't work.

One time in Montana's Absaroka-Beartooth Wilderness, I was hunting two bucks at dusk that regularly fed out of a thick stand of lodgepole pines high on a ridge. By the time they minced into the open, there wasn't light enough to make a sneak before dark. From my vantage point on an opposite ridge, however, it looked as though it might be possible to frighten them out of the timber and blowdowns where I thought they spent their days, across a ravine, and onto an open, grassy slope where I might get a shot. I wanted to be sure they didn't bolt before I was ready, so I pulled a classic sneak on the timber just as if it were the animal.

I approached the trees downwind of them, out of sight behind a rise, then crawled up to the timber. When I figured I was in just the right spot, I stood up and walked to the upwind side of the trees to let my scent drift in. Nothing happened. I tossed a few rocks into the trees. Still nothing. I tossed several more. Nothing. I talked to myself aloud, but nothing stirred in the dark, shadowy timber. *Hell, I thought, they're not there.* I walked into the trees to pick up their tracks and try to figure out what had happened. I hadn't gotten five yards into the thick mess of trees and fallen timber when they broke from just ahead. I hadn't expected them to still be there, so I wasn't ready for them. And by the time I'd fought my way out of the trees to a place where I could shoot, they were gone. Their tracks showed that they'd crossed the open slope just where I'd thought they would. Unfortunately I wasn't in the right place when they did it.

In a very large canyon, defined here as a canyon too big to shoot across from rim to rim, it's best to hunt it in sections, as if each part were a small canyon. In larger canyons the stands of trees are apt to be larger too. In such places pushing won't work as well, since most deer you frighten will simply run farther into the trees and up the canyon, cross the ridge, and disappear. Instead, you'll need to use a second strategy: still hunting and tracking.

It's best to still-hunt and track on the upper slope of a big stand of timber. Concentrate your still-hunting efforts along deer trails. Move upwind along the trail if possible, and remember that a trophy buck almost always will bed downwind of his backtrail, where he can smell and probably see you. Focus your attention on the downwind side of the trail, carry your gun at ready with your thumb near the safety, and stalk *slowly.* You've shifted from savanna hunting to hunting in timber again. After you've learned to recognize a big buck's track and strides, tracking works well in timber, or even on open slopes that lead into timber.

Pushing and still hunting and tracking are good strategies to use during the day when deer are bedded in timber or brush. A third method of combing a canyon for trophy bucks works best as early in the morning or as late in the evening as you can see. Move to a place where you're most likely to see deer, which means where deer come out of timber to feed or in feeding areas themselves. Since deer feed mainly on open slopes where the best browse grows, these are good places to catch deer both early, before they've returned to bedding areas in the trees, and late, after they've left beds.

Slopes where deer fed are best identified by tracks—the more the better. Also, look closely for cropped shrubs (the older the cut, the browner and more oxidized it will be) and forbs, and small plants that have been pulled up. It's useful to be able to identify browse plants, which include bitterbrush, mountain and curlleaf mahogany, cliffrose,

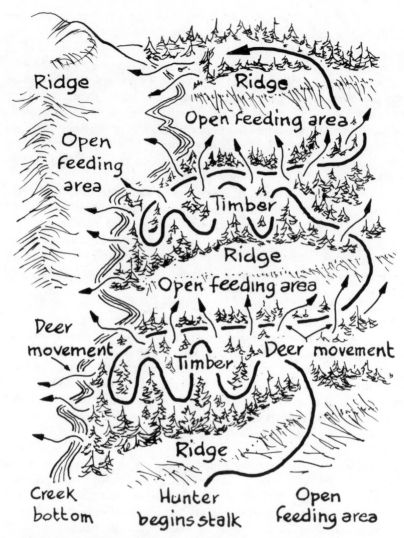

Combing a large canyon for mule deer. The goal here is to flush deer out of
the timber and onto the opposite, open slope (south- or southwest-facing), and
the hunter shoots across the canyon.

serviceberry, and wild rose. Muleys also feed on a variety of forbs and
the seedheads of certain grasses. Some open slopes—often because of
poor soil quality—may support little deer feed, while another slope in
the next ravine may be thick with it. Since early and late are prime
hunting periods, don't waste time with openings where deer aren't
feeding.

Trails that lead to and from bedding and feeding areas are good bets early and late, but you have to sneak up on them very carefully. If a buck knows you've approached a trail, he may not use it. Since most deer move into heavy cover when daylight nears, watch where a well-used trail disappears into timber. The older and wiser the buck, the

Another form of driving solo in a smaller canyon. Using your scent, which drifts up the canyon during the day when the air is warming and rising, you can frighten game up the ravine sides so you can get a shot.

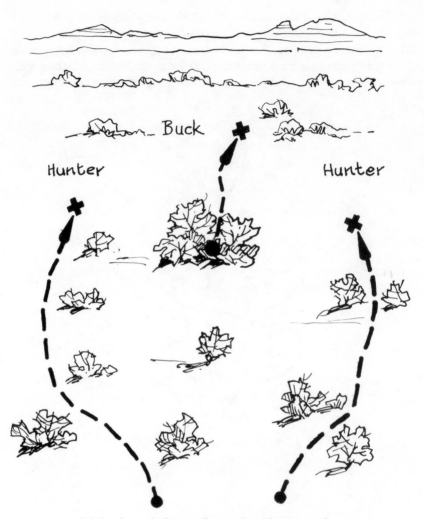

Driving for mule deer on flat terrain with a companion.

earlier he'll head for cover in the morning, and this is usually before it gets light. He won't normally show up in the open before it gets dark in the evening, either, especially in moderately to heavily hunted country. Once in a great while bucks get hungry early enough to show themselves before dark, and occasionally they'll stay out a bit late in the morning. Be sure to wait downwind, of course.

I've discovered a good canyon stalking technique and have practiced it for years. I'm sure other hunters also use this tactic. I call it the stop-pause-start (SPS) method. It's simply an exaggerated form of still hunting in which the stages are more drawn out. In regular still hunting, you move quietly and slowly through good deer country, stopping often to look and listen. The idea is to move slowly and quietly enough that you won't frighten deer or pass them by. In other words, still hunting increases your own awareness of what's out there. In a sense, SPS also serves to keep you aware, but its main function is to move what's there and hiding in such a way that you can get a shot.

SPS involves locating good-looking cover—then Stopping. Make some little commotion so that any buck will be aware of your presence and will have time to get nervous. Don't make too much commotion, however, since you don't want to frighten bucks farther up the canyon. Sneak up on each suspected cover as if you knew a deer was actually in it. Use the wind to your advantage, stay out of sight, and keep quiet.

The next step is the Pause stage, in which you wait. Don't hide— that defeats your purpose. Remain obvious, and wait. I usually wait at least thirty minutes. The pause stage is a good time to reminisce about the ones that got away, eat lunch, or just meditate, all the while keeping an eye on the suspected cover.

The last stage of SPS is Starting out again. Remember to fiddle around before leaving. At this point a buck will often become too nervous to stand it any longer. He's finally convinced he has been detected and will flee.

The really big mule bucks usually are nocturnal during hunting seasons, so if you want to get a shot at a good buck, you have to get him to leave his bed. Over my last few deer seasons, nearly 50 percent of all the bucks I saw were flushed by using SPS. The largest buck I've bagged since 1980—a huge, even- and heavy-antlered deer that scored 201 Boone-and-Crockett points green—was taken using SPS, although I did spend the better part of three days tracking him down before I was in a position to use the method.

As with any form of hunting, you don't use SPS just anywhere. You use it in a place where there's a fair chance that a good buck might be hiding and where you'll be able to get a shot if he is flushed. From my experience, the best places are ravines and small canyons of savanna vegetation, features that are blessedly plentiful in mule deer country.

Though it isn't properly stalking or sneaking, it's a good practice to return to a place where you've killed a trophy buck. That buck was there in the first place because of the area's good cover, feed, and remoteness, and because his big-antlered ancestors were there. And more often than not there will be other good deer in the country. Over the years I've taken nine big bucks off a certain plateau near the Wyoming-Utah border, many of them from almost the same spot on the plateau. A number of them had very similar antlers with a long, nontypical tine in exactly the same place, which indicates that they were related.

I discovered SPS for myself purely by accident, in a place that was perfectly suited for it. I'd been still-hunting up a long, steep canyon all morning. The vegetation was sparse on the steep, south-facing slope, with only an occasional thick patch of scrub oak or chokecherry. I'd skipped breakfast and my stomach had begun rumbling, so I sat down to eat lunch. Just across the ravine was a small patch of oak scrub that stood just about chest-high. The leaves had fallen and I

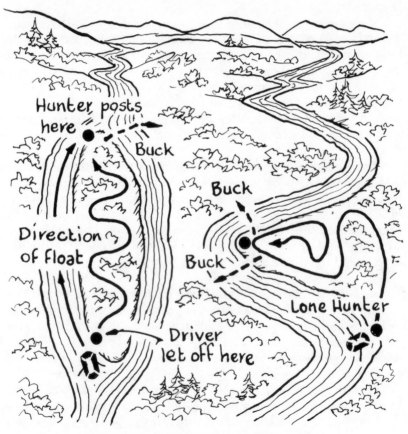

Driving tactics while float-hunting for mule deer.

Though still an experimental technique, rattling for mule deer does work at times, especially in a mature buck's center area during the rut. *Cheri Flory.*

could see into it pretty well, and I didn't see a thing. After lunch, roughly forty minutes later, I stood up, fumbled around for a few minutes as I got ready to hunt up the canyon, and then stepped out. At that moment a good buck bounded from the oak scrub and up the open slope. It was easy to collect him on that bare slope little more than a hundred yards away.

Though everything was purely coincidental that day, all the elements were there. I'd stopped at a likely place, I'd paused long enough that the buck became nervous, and I'd made a commotion before I started off. The commotion—at least in this case—was the kicker. It is often a key element in flushing a buck.

With the possible exception of hunting big rams on wilderness peaks, for my money there's nothing as remotely exciting as still-hunting, tracking, and stalking big mule deer bucks in timber. If I know there's a trophy buck bedded in a stand of trees, something in me tightens and my awareness sharpens. As I stalk slowly and quietly into the tangle of trees, I'm as alive as I ever get.

6

Wapiti
in the Trees

Classic western elk country is mountainous. Thick stands of timber
are broken by open grasslands. Traditionally elk, or wapiti, were
bagged as they fed out into the open from the trees in the evening or
early in the morning. Now it seems that elk show themselves less
during daylight hours. They still feed in the open grasslands, but like
wise and hunted mule deer bucks, they've become more nocturnal
during hunting seasons. This is true even during the rut, at which
time they're supposedly more foolish. Hunting elk has changed over
the years, then, from mostly an open-country proposition to one in
thick trees. Tactics have shifted from spotting, sneaking, and long-
range shooting to still hunting, tracking, and quick, short-range shots.
More and more, hunters have to go into the trees to collect a trophy
bull.

   Elk calls (artificial bugles) aren't terribly effective in bringing bulls
to the hunter, in spite of advertisements and magazine articles to the
contrary. They are good for locating bulls, however, and then a sneak
can be planned and executed. Elk rut during the last half of September and slightly into October. I spent eight seasons studying elk be-

havior while a graduate student in wildlife biology, and I found the peak of rutting intensity to be about September 22. Weather has something to do with it: Hot and dry conditions reduce rutting intensity and frequency, and cold weather, especially accompanied by storms, accelerates it.

Although it's true that bull elk become more foolish during the rut, big harem bulls are accompanied by as many as two dozen cows that don't get addled during breeding season. Thus instead of stalking one lovesick bull, you're actually attempting to sneak up on a score of sets of keen ears, eyes, and noses. It's a rough stalk, but it's always exciting.

If I'm hunting during the rut these days, I try a good-quality artificial bugle call first. I don't expect a trophy bull to come crashing in, though it has happened once, which always keeps me hopeful. I bugle several times to get a bull to answer, then I stalk the bugling bull. Again, the stalk or sneak begins before I actually sight the animal. I circle downwind first—an elk has a sense of smell like a bloodhound's. I wear wool and, if the weather is appropriate, sneakers or moccasins when sneaking through trees—elk can hear nearly as well as mule deer. If there's no snow on the ground, I make the last part of the stalk and sneak in stocking feet. I use my artificial bugle no more than necessary—just enough to keep the bull pinpointed. As I get closer, I call at a much reduced volume. Sometimes an elk may bugle often enough that you don't have to use an artificial call and can just stalk the vocalizing bull.

There are two types of adult bulls during the rut: the herd bulls, or "harem masters," and the bulls that hang around the periphery of the herd and make life miserable for the herd bull, or "outriders." Harem masters keep a group of cows in a small area by herding, threatening, and other antics. Outriders are usually smaller adults that hang around the harem in hopes of stealing off with a cow or two while the herd bull is busy elsewhere or of moving in and defeating the herd bull as the rigors of rutting take their toll on his strength, as they inevitably will. Harem masters will rarely come to an artificial bugle, or for that matter, a real one. They have their girlfriends in hand, so they have little to gain and an awful lot to lose by approaching something unknown in the bush. Outriders will sometimes approach an artificial bugle, but more often than not to them your call represents another bachelor, so going to you is a waste of time. They're more likely to approach a cow call.

Yearlings and two-year-old bulls will sometimes approach either type of call out of curiosity, and if you're just after meat, this is a good way to get it. I've bagged three or four young, tender-meat bulls over the years using this method.

The very first elk I killed was a yearling bull that answered, after a fashion, my aluminum pipe call and then came part way in. His "bugle" was mostly squeak and squawk and reminded me of a novice violin player practicing "Clementine." It bore only the remotest resemblance to the bugle of a big, barrel-chested herd bull. The yearling answered most of my vocalizing but was tentative about coming in. So I stalked in his direction, occasionally bugling at him. He squawked back, I stalked on, and when I looked around a big fir tree, there he was standing in the ravine bottom. One shot settled him, and he was a delicious chunk of meat.

During the rut, then, the best way to collect a *good* bull is to either stalk a vocalizing bull, as already mentioned, or stalk a favorite rutting area. I've spent several elk seasons stalking through a particular meadow and forest or on a mountainside because I knew from sign that a herd was using the place and that a big bull was there too.

Once, in southern Montana's Hellroaring Creek drainage, I found a herd of elk that seemed to stay at the end of a steep and thick creek. At the head of the creek was an open basin where they fed, usually late in the evening just before dark. They fed back in the trees as soon as it began to get light, and if I wanted to kill an elk during the daytime, I had to plan to sneak up on it through tangles of blowdowns and timber. It looked to be a hopeless option, especially with as many elk as there were—I counted thirty one evening. It seemed best to stay with stalking and watching in the open basin, even though they were there for such a brief time during daylight hours.

I waited one morning before dawn at the edge of a meadow thick with tracks, rubbed saplings, droppings, and grazed and browsed vegetation. It was well below freezing, and I scrunched back beneath a lodgepole pine to get out of the breeze. The herd bull was answering another, distant bugle from across the basin somewhere, so I decided to stalk toward him even though I couldn't see a thing in the coal-mine darkness. I walked very slowly across the meadow, trying not to stumble over saplings or step in the small creeks that trickled through it. I hoped I wouldn't blunder into one of the grazing elk.

The light came slowly. Finally I could make out the shadows of saplings and burnt stumps, then the eastern horizon began to lighten and color. The bugle echoed back and forth across the meadow, followed by deep, rasping grunts. I hadn't frightened any elk, the wind seemed more or less steady into my face, and I was closing. I found a place behind a cluster of shin-tangle and waited.

Elk in typical forest and meadow habitat.

I thought the elk were close: Twice I scented their musky odor, and once I believed I heard one walking off. The light comes slowly when you're waiting for it, but finally—after what seemed at least a decade—I could see some cows moving slowly into the trees two hundred yards away. More cows ghosted across the meadow and into the pines, and then I could see antlers. The bull was behind other cows as they fed into the trees, however, and I never did get a shot at him. But stalking a meadow, ravine, or mountainside where a herd of elk is feeding and living during the rut can sometimes be effective.

When you are looking for an elk herd's hangout, watch for tracks, cropped vegetation, antler rubs, droppings, beds, and other sign. Always keep aware of the wind, stalk silently, and stay out of sight. Your gun shouldn't be hanging from your shoulder. Keep it ready and stalk either the bugling bull or the area as you would a covey of quail—with your thumb on the safety.

Over the years I've collected several mature bulls by stalking their bugling. One of the most typical stalks happened about half a dozen seasons ago. I'd heard the bulls (there were two, which hinted strongly that they were outriders or bachelor bulls, not herd bulls) before dawn, and I'd climbed a steep ridge in their direction in the darkness. Then they stopped bugling. I sat on the crest of the pass and listened, hoping they'd start again but fearing they had moved off. The eastern horizon turned from gray to turquoise to gold to wine, and still they didn't sound off. I pressed the bugle to my lips and blew: *e-e-e-e-e-E−E−E−E---ungh-ungh*. From across the basin, one of the bulls answered, and a moment after, so did the other.

I moved down from the crest into the timber, then circled to get the wind from them to me. They bugled again without prompting, and I homed in on them. They were nearly a mile away, I guessed, in a thick stand of lodgepole pines on the other side of a sheer limestone cliff at the far edge of the basin. I stalked on, trying to get my bearing in the trees from a big, snow-covered peak to the west and from the wind direction. I hoped the bulls would bugle without any of my own calling. They didn't, however, and I moved slowly through the timber toward where I hoped they still were hiding. Eventually I called again. Both bulls answered immediately and at almost the same time, and they *were* closer. I altered my course slightly to again home in on them and stalked on.

I kept to this course, occasionally orienting myself by the mountain peak, but the bulls remained silent and I became unsure once more. Again I bugled, and a bull answered off to my left, then another from just ahead. They were no more than two hundred yards away in the thick trees, and I could hear the splintering of branches as one bull battered an unfortunate sapling with his antlers. I decided to go for the one on the left. The wind was slightly more favorable in that direction, and he seemed less tentative and more angry in his bugling and antler thrashing, so I figured he would be less likely to spook if I made a mistake.

I took off my boots and hung them around my neck, double-checked to be sure there was a round in the chamber, dropped a pinch of Sahara-dry pine-needle duff to check the wind, and eased ahead. I strained to see into the shadows and to hear anything that might hint at the bull's exact location. Occasionally I heard faint cracklings in the brush ahead, and once I caught a whiff of the unmistakable musky pungency of a rutting bull elk. My thumb was on the safety, and my heart pounded so loudly I was sure the elk could hear it.

The final part of the stalk—the sneak—is always the most exciting, even though you may not even have seen the animal you're after. I tried to calm myself, to slow my pounding heart, to ease the mule kicking in my gut, before the moment of truth. I didn't dare bugle again at such close range for fear of making a mistake and sending the bull off into the next drainage. I concentrated on the wind, on moving quietly, on looking ahead, and strangely I became calm yet ready. And there was something ahead—a piece of rotten blowdown, perhaps, but it wasn't quite the right color. I put the scope on it, and it moved almost inperceptibly. Then the breeze rippled a bit of dark mane fur. I made out where the neck joined the chest and moved the cross hairs to the spot almost automatically as I pulled the trigger. The bull was a fair, though not extraordinary, 6 by 6.

After the rut, adult bulls leave the harems and retreat to remote, thick country well away from roads and trails. They've lost a lot of weight during the rut, especially herd bulls, and in order to survive the winter they have to gain at least some of it back before the heavy snows. To do that, they have to find good feed, cover, and water within close proximity, and they can't be chivied about by hunters. Behaviorally, adult bulls go from brawling playboys to monks within a matter of days.

If you're unfamiliar with the area you'll be hunting, the best way to find "elk holes" is to use a topographical map to locate isolated gorges, hanging basins, or high ridges that are well away from roads or much-used trails (many national forest and even wilderness horse trails resemble freeways during elk season). Still hunting, tracking, and ambushing are all good tactics. Once you've found an elk hole, you can determine if a bull is using the place by sign, or spoor, such as droppings, tracks, antler rubs, wallows, cropped vegetation, and beds. If you know where a bull feeds, try ambushing him as he feeds out of cover early or late. Often bulls feel secure in their isolation and will feed in the open at dawn and dusk.

If the bull isn't feeding in the open when it's light enough to shoot, still-hunt or track into his cover much as you would into a mule deer buck's center area. Move slowly and quietly, into the wind if possible. Again, wear quiet clothing such as wool and stalk more slowly than an octogenarian inchworm. Watch on the downwind side of the trail; a wise veteran bull will bed where he can scent and see his backtrail. Trust your nose when you're close to a bull. They have a strong, musky odor that you'll recognize when you get a snootful. Keep your gun ready and in your hands, never hanging from your shoulder: When you see the bull he will be very near.

You can ambush a bull elk at a mid- or late-season elk hole in the early morning before sunrise, or after sunset, when the air is cool, dense, and drifting downhill. The hunter waits on an open slope above the feeding area near where the elk leaves the timber.

I've collected several midseason bulls by stalking into elk holes. It does require patience, both in finding an elk hole and in determining what the bull is doing—whether he is feeding into the open during daylight, and where, or is staying holed up in cover until nightfall—as well as in sneaking into the tangle after him. If you're fortunate enough to find an elk hole, return again next season. Do so even if you've killed a bull there; chances are that he was there because it's a perfect place for hiding and putting on weight without being disturbed, and it's likely that another bull will be there next year.

During the midseason bulls do sometimes give themselves away by bugling. In fact, bulls have been known to bugle at about any time of year, although they do so most frequently around the rut. I found at least one elk hole by stalking a bugle in mid-October. I heard the bull in northern Utah's Wasatch Mountains one morning as I stood around

Still hunting into a suspected elk hole in search of bedded elk or ambushing an elk near a feeding area. If the wind is up canyon during the day, the hunter starts at the top of the elk hole.

This is a fair, but not outstanding, 6 by 6 bull I took recently. He's thin because the rut has just ended.

the campfire shifting a too-hot tin cup of tea from hand to hand in the predawn darkness. My horse whinnied in response from the end of her tether. That bugle gave me direction for the day's stalking.

I found the elk hole in a hanging basin late that morning, and from the sign, the bull had been there for some time. There were big, blunt-tipped hoofprints, cropped chokecherry and serviceberry bushes, grazed grasses in the creekside meadow, droppings, and a well-used trail that disappeared into the shadows of big fir and spruce trees, aspen saplings, and brush. I waited above on the slope that evening and again in the morning, but nothing showed. Then I still-hunted along the trail into the thick tangle of blowdowns, timber, and brush, hoping for the best. I stopped often to look and listen, keeping the .270 ready and in my hands. Every time I hunt that way, I'm amazed all over again at how truly exciting it gets. You become more aware than you ever would be otherwise.

Then the bull was suddenly up and over a blowdown, the sunlight glinting briefly off big, ivory-tipped antlers, and he was bounding across the trail. There was a shot, though I didn't remember taking it. I rushed to where I'd last seen him, and big, deeply cut, easy-to-follow tracks led off into the trees. A few yards down the trail I found a drop of bright, frothy lung blood on a fallen aspen leaf, and then another drop and more where he'd blown onto chest-high trees. I rounded a blowdown he'd jumped, crawled under the boughs of a fir, and there he was, stretched out as if in full stride.

During the late season, in November and December, bulls have regained some of the weight lost during the rut and are better able to face a hard winter. If there's been heavy snow, bigger bulls will tend to stay in remote lower places such as gorges or even wooded marshes where hunters can't get at them. They may also retreat to high ridges where the wind sweeps the snow away and they can get at feed.

To find them, try to think like a bull. Where would you go that you could get away from hunters yet still be able to find food? If there's snow on the ground, long-distance spotting can be productive; use good binoculars or a spotting scope. Tracking may be effective and easy on snow, but it's important to know the difference between old and fresh tracks. Make tracks of your own and examine them to see what tracks look like fresh; check them in a day or two to learn how older tracks appear. Odds are that the only large hoofprints you'll see other than the elk's will be that of a moose, and those are larger, more heart-shaped, and pointed at the tips.

If you track, you won't always be fortunate enough to do it into the wind. If the wind is quartering from behind you or coming from the side, make loops downwind from the trail, returning to it every few hundred yards for confirmation. If the wind is from directly behind you, circle well ahead and then return to where you think the trail went. Repeat the manuever if you were right. Remember that elk have excellent vision, and on snow an upright animal in anything but white camouflage is very obvious at even a great distance.

Throughout the hunting seasons a bull elk is a changeable beast, and to consistently take one you must use different tactics at different times. You have to be just as adjustable and fluid in your hunting as a bull elk is in his living habits.

7

Moose Magic

The moose is the largest member of the deer family and grows the biggest antlers. A big Alaskan bull moose is one of the world's most impressive trophies. Moose are found from the forests of Maine to the high basins of the Rockies, and north through dense coniferous forests in Canada to tundra barrens well above the Arctic Circle.

A large Alaska-Yukon bull moose may exceed a ton on the hoof and eat seventy-five pounds of vegetation a day. Naturalist Adolph Murie tells of an Indian named Big Charlie who killed a large bull moose along the Koyukuk River in northern Alaska. Instead of packing the meat to the village, Big Charlie moved his family to the moose and pitched a tent over it. They feasted many days. When they returned to the village a month later, Big Charlie said his wife had a sore stomach.

Moose meat is among the best in North America. I'd rate it second only to fresh Dall sheep (I think it's slightly better than eland, which is generally the favorite African wild meat). I hunt moose far north of my cabin at least as much for the food as for the trophy.

Moose populations farthest north may begin rutting early in September, and even those farthest to the south in Wyoming and Utah have begun to rut by late September. In both places they may continue rutting into October. Bull moose during the rut behave more like rutting mule deer than elk do: They consort with one cow when she's in or approaching estrus, and then it's off to find another comely cow. Moose tend to be more foolish than the heavily hunted and manwise mule deer, though this is not quite so true where they themselves are heavily hunted. I hunted them in the sixties in central British Columbia, where they were heavily chivied about by Indians from the local Canim Lake Reserve. These moose were as cagey as whitetails.

Moose, along with the mule deer, have perhaps the best combination of senses in the deer family. Their senses of smell and hearing have long been recognized by hunters as very keen, but for some reason their eyesight has been discounted. Possibly this was because most moose were hunted in thick trees, and it was sometimes possible for the stalker to get very close and then assume he had done so because moose couldn't see well.

While hunting moose, I've had several encounters that taught me all too well not to underestimate their vision. Once I was walking down a game trail through thick aspens. Leaves were still on the trees, and my vision was limited to twenty-five yards. I heard something coming up the trail toward me. The breeze was drifting into my face, so I didn't have to worry that whatever was coming would catch my scent. I eased above the trail and waited. Eventually I spotted the black withers of a moose as he browsed in the brush below. Then an antler soared above the scrub. The bull was twenty yards away. He stepped through the saplings and into the open as I slowly and carefully raised the rifle. The bull saw the motion when I had the rifle halfway to my shoulder, so I stopped and waited. The bull continued to stare until my arms began to shake in that unnatural position. I couldn't hold it any longer, so I eased the rifle up again. The bull whirled and disappeared.

Another time I was stalking toward a basin where I'd seen some bulls during preseason scouting. I crawled across a ridge, using brush to break my outline. Perhaps three hundred yards away across the draw stood a good bull. He'd already spotted me and was staring hard in my direction. He saw the small movement as I brought the rifle around, and he took off into heavy timber before I could shoot.

The moose's sense of smell is even better than its vision. I had three bulls wind me at nearly a mile in some Arctic mountains. And its hearing is just as good. I once tried a sneak on a big bull bedded in a thick patch of spruce across an Alaskan river. My companion settled down on the bluff half a mile away to watch. I rowed the raft quietly across the river, tied it off in an eddy, and walked onto the tundra. The wind was from the bull and into my face, so he couldn't scent me, and I was out of sight in the trees, so he couldn't see me. My companion later told me the bull took off soon after I'd stepped out of the raft, so the moose had to have heard me, though I don't remember making the slightest sound. So when stalking moose, whether on the open tundra or in thick timber, stay out of sight, keep downwind, and move as silently as a leopard.

Hunting moose during the rut is probably the most exciting time and, if it's done correctly, the most productive. Both cows and bulls are vocal during the rut. Cow moose moan something like Herefords on a Wyoming prairie might when they're in or approaching heat. Bulls grunt and have a deep, nasal call something like *O-O-O-O-O-o-o-o-o-o-k-k-k-k-k-gh*, repeated two to five times. Though there are both bull and cow call on the market, I seem to have the most luck just imitating them vocally. In any case, you must listen to and study a moose's calling and grunting before you'll get it right.

Bull moose sparring in early September just before the rut.

Unlike bull elk these days, bull moose, at least those that haven't been shot at, do come to a bull call. If a bull moose has an estrous cow with him, however, he probably won't come in to your call; then you'll need to stalk him just as you would a bugling bull elk. Chances are that even if he won't come to your call, he will answer it, so you can stalk his vocalizing. One guide from the Yukon makes a remarkably effective call from a plastic bleach jug with a length of twine run through a small hole in its bottom. The sound is made by tugging the twine through the hole, and it does bring in bulls.

Moose have a low volume-to-surface-area ratio, as well as a dark color (Shiras moose are quite black), which makes them susceptible to overheating. It also allows them to inhabit some of the coldest country on the continent. As a result, moose are normally inactive during the day, except on cloudy or cold days or after a prolonged period of storm when they are especially hungry. To successfully hunt moose, it's often necessary to stalk into the cool shadows of timber or brush, where they bed and spend most of their daylight hours. Because of their acute senses, if bulls are in timber, it's tough to get close enough for a shot. One thing that's in the hunter's favor, however, is that moose are often hunted under wilderness conditions and can be naive about the intentions of people with guns. A healthy moose has little to fear, not even wolves, since they're too big, tough, and fast. So they often won't run from something unknown, and if they're unfamiliar with the scent or sight of man they may let you approach close enough for a shot. Again, this definitely isn't the case if they've been hunted much.

On my first moose hunt in central British Columbia, the bulls had been hunted heavily. They hung to the thick spruce and poplar forests, and they were almost impossible to get up on. They'd been hunted extensively by the locals, and they were too well aware of what man meant. The only decent bull I saw on that hunt was one we tracked to a heavy tangle of willows. We'd been very quiet on the new, soft snow, the wind had been favorable all morning, and at that instant it was blowing from the willows to us. A small branch snapped under my foot, but it was muffled by the snow and I barely heard it. The bull, a hundred yards away in brush, heard it though and was up and off before I could bring the rifle up. We followed his tracks for several hours, and later in the day he got on our backtrail and left the valley. I came away from that hunt without a moose but with a new respect for their wariness.

From my tales of unsuccessful stalks you may have decided that bull moose are nearly mythical creatures that are seldom brought to

The fruits of my first solo Arctic wilderness hunt, which I made for four weeks in 1981.

bag, so let me tell you about a successful moose stalk. In 1981 I'd been alone for a month and hunting along a very remote Arctic river for several weeks without so much as a glimpse of a bull moose. I'd about given up and was only going through the routine of hunting because I had nothing better to do. I had already bagged a good caribou earlier in the hunt, so I had a good trophy and meat to survive on; it didn't really matter if I bagged a moose. I'd walk along the river each morning and afternoon, enjoying the Indian summer, the cackling geese winging their way south in high chevrons, and the haunting wail of Arctic loons. From time to time I'd hike out onto the rolling tundra hills to gather a quart of overripe blueberries. It was an idyllic existence, moose or no.

One evening as I was sitting beside the rushing river, contemplating the large grayling that were sucking tiny, black mayflies from a pool, I heard a bull moose call from the timber. I'd already made up my mind to take any bull I had a crack at, so I stalked toward the sound, careful about my footing on the river gravel, aware the wind was favorable. I could hear the crackling of branches as the bull smashed a willow with his antlers. I moved as carefully as I knew how, determined not to spook him off. Eventually I was within fifty yards. I couldn't see him through the thick willows, but each time he smashed at one with his antlers I could see its top sway and snap violently. I didn't think I could get through the tangle quietly, so I imitated his call and grunt. The bull answered immediately, smashed at another hapless willow, and trotted into the open with blood in his eye. I was astonished at his size; it took three .270 bullets into his shoulder at thirty yards to put him down. He had a 65-inch spread, long and broad palms, and 27 long points, and he scored several points above the Boone-and-Crockett minimum.

After the rut, moose bulls form bachelor groups or go off by themselves. Like elk, they lose some weight during the rut (though not as much as elk normally do), and also like elk, they have to put some of it back on in order to survive the winter. Moose and elk both finish rutting early enough in the fall that they have time to regain some of their weight before winter. Mule deer, on the other hand, aren't so fortunate; they rut very late in the autumn, and winter may come during the rut, so they don't regain much of the weight they lost while chasing does about the mountains and woods. In mule country that typically has severe winters, adult bucks suffer the highest winterkill.

If bull moose form bachelor bands after the rut—and where there are enough bulls, they usually do—they frequently spar. This involves banging antlers and pushing one another around. The sounds of clattering antlers can be heard for miles across the silent, lonely valleys and barrens, especially early in the morning when the air is still. I once guided a friend after Shiras moose in northern Utah after he'd been lucky enough to draw one of the few permits. We heard the unmistakable clash of antlers from a mile across Magpie Canyon, and we stalked it. We circled to keep downwind, eased through the brush quietly, and stayed out of sight. We had the pick of five bulls that were browsing and playfully pushing one another about across the ravine, and my friend made the shot count.

If there's snow on the ground after the rut, spotting bulls from a distance and then sneaking up on them is a top tactic. The large, dark moose are very conspicuous against snow from a distance, especially from across a canyon or from an elevation. At the same time, unless you're in white camo, you'll be just as conspicuous to the moose.

High-school baseball star R.W. Lovell, the son of my best hunting chum, with the Shiras moose I guided him to. If it looks like we're holding the antlers on, we are. They fell off when the bull was shot (he was ready to shed anyway). I'm the one with the ice on his beard, by the way.

Pulling off the sneak is the tough part; never underestimate a moose's senses.

Over the seasons of successes and failures in stalking moose, I've come up with a few general rules. A bull moose is highly heat sensitive. I've often come across bulls, even in the arctic where it's usually cold during the rut, lying in wallows or shallow streams. Because of their heat sensitivity, moose generally bed in thick timber or brush. With their extraordinary senses, they are especially adapted for it, too. They dislike direct sunlight, so they are nocturnal or crepuscular (active in the dawn and dusk hours), though they will move about on cloudy and cool days. The hunter will frequently have to stalk into timber to collect a bull, and to do that he must wear quiet clothing and footgear. He also must be aware of wind direction. If he jumps a moose in timber, it's going to be close and any shooting has to be quick. If everything falls into place, the hunter may bag a trophy bull. Then the work begins. You'll see that Big Charlie up on the Koyukuk had the right idea.

8

Black Bears

Most of my experience with black bears has been in the Great North, from central British Columbia on the Cariboo Plateau north to well above the Arctic Circle. In my experience, black bears are primarily creatures of the forest. Even on backpacking trips in the mountains of southern Arizona and New Mexico, I noticed that blackies hung to the high, forested peaks of the Chiricahuas, Huachucas, and Gilas, as did those in the mountains of northeastern Sonora in Mexico. But though they are primarily forest animals, I've also seen them frequenting high, above-timberline basins in Wyoming, Idaho, and Montana; browsing on lowbush blueberries on barren tundra hills; scavenging on open beaches in southern coastal Alaska; and grazing in old burns in backcountry Canada. Just the same, I think of black bears as creatures of the forest.

Bears, both blacks and grizzlies, are hunted in either the spring or the fall. If they're hunted during the fall, they're usually bagged by elk or deer hunters, not by people who are after bears specifically. In the spring, however, nothing else is hunted, so hunters out then are after bears only and are apt to be a bit more knowledgeable about their habits.

Most spring bear hunts open around the first of April, a time when the snow either is beginning to melt or is pretty well gone. The key to stalking at this time is to learn what bears just out of hibernation are likely to feed on and then watching those areas. In Idaho and Montana I've found spring bears feeding on the earliest grasses, especially on bare, exposed slopes and meadows. Later in the spring they feed on grasses, sedges, and a variety of succulent forbs, annuals, and perennials. In piñon forests in the southeast they search out pinecones for the pine nuts. I believe they do this with other species of pines also, especially southern ponderosa pine.

In the Arctic or Far North there may still be quite a bit of snow on the ground and very little plant growth when bears emerge from hibernation. Here bears feed on rose hips, crowberries, cranberries, blueberries, and other berries left from the season before. They also feed on peavine roots extensively in places where these grow. You can tell if bears are using these because they roll up the turf to a depth of a few inches to expose the roots. Where they're feeding heavily on roots, the topsoil may have been rolled up in this manner over many acres.

Bears also search out winter-killed big-game animals. I've watched black bears systematically search ravines near the border of Yellowstone National Park in the spring looking for elk, moose, deer, or bighorn sheep that have died during the winter and been covered and frozen by the snows. I've seen them do the same thing north of the Arctic Circle, and I once observed two black bears working on a caribou carcass frozen in a river. Apparently the bull caribou had fallen through the ice while crossing and couldn't get out.

I've accompanied friends on several spring bear hunts in Idaho and Montana, and in the places we've gone – the Salmon River Primitive Area in Idaho and the Absaroka-Beartooth Wilderness Area of Montana – the best and most accepted way was glassing open slopes from a distance and then sneaking up on a bear. On the first trip in Idaho, twenty-five years ago, we spotted a bear across a long canyon. It was midmorning, and the sun had been up long enough that the air had warmed and was drifting uphill. We circled up to the head of the canyon to be above and downwind of the bear, crossed the creek a mile above the opening, then eased down the slope toward it. We were aware that bears have keen hearing, but like most readers of hunting magazines and books, we believed they had terrible eyesight.

We reached the edge of the meadow, which was a half mile wide, and eased through the sedges, brambles, saplings, and nettles toward where we'd seen the bear. He was there, all right – we saw his back above the luxuriant, green herbage as he grazed. The wind was right, and it wasn't difficult to sneak quietly through the grasses on the wet soil. The bear took a routine look around as we stalked toward him, and even though we were more than a quarter mile away and half-hidden in the vegetation, he saw us. Neither of us had expected the bear to see us at that distance. He stood on hind legs and looked harder, then whirled and disappeared in the trees. So much for the idea that bears have poor eyesight!

Hunting blackies in the autumn is less predictable than hunting them in spring. While certain feed plants, wild rose hips for example, will concentrate black bears, and late salmon runs can do the same, most black bears in fall are killed by hunters out for other game, like deer, elk, or moose.

The first time I hunted black bears it was late in the season, mid-November, in central British Columbia around Crooked Lake. Like most fall bear hunters I'd been out after moose and goats, but the outfitter found a big track and was eager to loose his pack of black-and-tans and Walkers on it. It wasn't long before the dogs caught up with the bear and began the chase. After a few miles they had the big bruin treed, but as soon as we approached the immense fir, the bear descended without touching it and was quickly through the astonished dogs and off again. The same thing happened four more times, and we lost one dog in the process: The bear took a swipe at it on his way off and drove a rib through its lungs.

The next time the hounds treed the bear, we had a conference. We decided it might be best if only one of us approached the tree, sneaking up on it from downwind, staying out of sight, moving as silently as possible on the heavy, wet snow. I did just that, spotting the bear at least a hundred feet up in an immense spruce. Then I found another tree with a fork at just the right height for a rifle rest and eased the gun up. Unfortunately the bear saw the movement and went down that tree as fast as gravity would allow, and we were off again. We realized that in order to get close enough for a shot, one of us had to stalk the tree the bear was in as if the tree itself were the quarry. My second stalk went pretty similarly to the first one, and the bruin escaped again. The next time, however, things were a bit different.

I eased down the slope silently in the quiet snow, out of sight behind a screen of saplings, the wind more or less into my face. The hounds were leaping and baying at the base of the tree, but I couldn't see the bear, though I knew he was somewhere above. I eased lower down the slope, then to my left, but I still couldn't spot the bear. I moved around more, then I went through the upper branches carefully with my rifle scope. There was no sign of a bear—until I reached the very top. The treetop had apparently been blasted off by lightning years earlier and had also been hollowed out, perhaps by burning from the lightning or maybe from rotting. I spotted a small patch of black fur at the top of the hollow—although nothing I could shoot at— so I knew the wily bear was hiding there. One of my Indian guides wanted me to shoot the bear through the side of the tree, but that didn't seem quite fair somehow; and even if I killed it, we'd have the devil's own time getting the bear out of the hollow. That was one of many that got away.

As with stalking many other types of game, it's often necessary to sneak up on the place where a bear feeds, especially in timber or heavy brush, rather than on the bear itself. I found this to be true along the salmon streams draining Alaska's southern coast. Along almost any stream that salmon spawn in—and they do in most river and creeks there (at least they did until the *Valdez* oil spill)—bears have favorite places where fish are the easiest to catch or where they congregate, such as below falls or rapids or in long shallows. Bears trample down surrounding vegetation, and these places are often very open. One of the best ways to take a black bear is to find such a place, determine prevailing wind directions at various times of day, learn where bears approach from, then stalk the feeding area. I've done it successfully, more often for photos than for hunting. If you are careful, you can occasionally get up on a good bear.

The last time I tried it was on a tributary of the Copper River in southern Alaska. I had found the place while hiking earlier in the spring before the salmon had started migrating upriver. From the number of dried fish heads and skeletons and old bear and eagle scats from the previous year, I was sure that I'd find a bear or two once the fish put in their annual appearance. I came back a week after the migration had passed the mouth of the creek and, sure enough, found all kinds of bear sign. I wasn't really interested in shooting a bear with anything but a camera. I got a couple of good photos of small bears, but I wanted a real trophy, so I kept at it.

I knew there was one big black bear feeding at the pool, but from the tracks, I could tell there was also a big coastal grizzly. The best and quickest way to tell grizzly from black bear tracks is to examine the foreprints. With a grizzly, the claws are always evident and print well ahead of the toes, but with a black bear, the claws print close to the toes or may not show up at all.

The presence of the big grizzly made me nervous, so the next time in I carried a shotgun loaded with 00 buckshot. It was a good thing I did, because I parted some of that thick, streamside brush and came face-to-face with the very dark grizzly. He *woofed* and I backed up. He *woofed* again, this time with less surprise and more anger, and I looked around quickly for a tree to climb. I was well up a spruce I hoped he couldn't knock over by the time he *woofed* one last time. Fortunately the bear decided I was no threat—or maybe he decided I was too much of one—and he turned and walked off into the alder tangle. I didn't get a photo of the big black, but I consider myself lucky not to have gotten into more trouble than I did with the grizzly.

Of all the methods I've used for stalking black bears, either with a camera or a gun, I prefer tracking, especially on snow. I first tried it while hunting elk and bighorn sheep in Montana's Absaroka-Beartooth Wilderness. I was camped in Hummingbird Basin at nine thousand feet. The evening before opening morning a snowstorm swept through and dumped a foot of light, cold snow. There was a clear, blue, icy sky the next morning, and bear tracks ran right through camp. My saddle mare had had a fit the night before, and at the time I'd thought it was because of the wind ripping through the pines.

I decided to follow the bear tracks. They weren't particularly big tracks, but the exercise would be fun, and anyway, they were likely to go where elk were. By late morning the sun was melting the new snow, and it was dropping from the laden boughs in great glops on the bear's trail. The tracks disappeared in the timber. I gave it up and went to look for more promising elk country. I did get a 6-by-6 bull that morning after tracking him to a tangle of pines. I circled to see if he'd left the stand, and when I found he hadn't, I still-hunted into the trees until I killed him at thirty yards as he stood up from his bed.

Several days later, while looking for rams, I came across the bear's trail again. It had snowed once more, and the tracks were fresh. I followed them through a stand of lodgepole pines, over a ridge where the bear had torn apart a rotten blowdown searching for ant eggs, down a slope, across a creek, and into another drainage, where at dusk I spotted him busily digging up an anthill. I circled to be more securely downwind, found some pine saplings for cover (I hadn't forgotten the lesson I'd learned while stalking that Idaho bruin), and approached quietly. I closed to about fifty yards, rested the rifle across a tree branch, and in the end decided not to shoot. He wasn't a big bear, though he did have a pretty cinnamon coat.

In Saskatchewan, where I've hunted white-tailed deer, black bears are most frequently shot over a bait. The most common form of baiting is using a thirty- or fifty-five-gallon steel drum with a slot cut in its side so a bear can get its front paw into the honey or whatever bait is inside. A hunter waits in a nearby tree stand, then pots the hapless bear. That kind of hunt doesn't appeal to me and I haven't tried it, though it does seem to be a successful method. I suppose it's true that a hunter must stalk the tree stand as he would a bear, coming from downwind and staying silent, but those I know who have tried it don't rate the whole experience very highly.

Bears have very keen hearing and arguably the best sense of smell of any game animal. I once watched a bear through binoculars stop to ponder my trail in a valley a mile below. I'd trekked up the canyon two days earlier, and it had rained since then, but the bear apparently could smell me anyway. Although it's true that vision is the bear's weakest sense, and that mule deer, pronghorns, sheep, elk, and other animals see better, this knowledge unfortunately has made too many hunters underestimate a black bear's vision, with the result that the bear sees them and takes off. Thus, when stalking a bear, never show yourself in the open if at all possible, move into the wind, and be very quiet.

Except in rare instances, black bears aren't dangerous, so you won't get the gut-wrenching, heart-pounding, sweaty excitement you would when stalking a grizzly. But there's another, quieter, kind of feeling when you sneak up within close range of a good, fat blackie. It's one of a job well done, of being good enough to get close to an animal that can scent as well as any, hear among the best, and see adequately enough. This alone makes the black bear an outstanding trophy.

9

The Wily Whitetail

I haven't had as much experience hunting white-tailed deer as I have with mule deer, elk, moose, pronghorn, and mountain sheep, and there are probably many hunters who know more than I do about whitetail hunting. But as a game biologist, I may be able to offer a different perspective.

My hunting for whitetails has been limited to the west, from Saskatchewan to Arizona, and much of my experience has been gained when I was after mule deer. Back in the seventies, I even passed up a good whitetail buck in western Wyoming because I wanted a big muley, although I'd already killed scores of trophy mule deer. Some of my Wyoming hosts felt the same way. Curious, isn't it?

The difference between the two species lies primarily in temperament. Whitetails are high-strung, but mule deer are calm and collected. Whitetails lie low when hunters pour into the countryside; mule deer, on the other hand, will usually abandon their routines and head for the steepest canyons, thickest brush, and most remote country they can find—at least veteran and man-wise bucks will. (In spite of a big school of thought to the contrary, the mule deer is as smart and, where he's been close to man and his activities, as man-wise as the whitetail.) Whitetails frequently live closer to man, even in farm and ranch backyards, and are used to people wandering through their range. Their routines usually aren't as easily broken. And an animal with more fixed routines is easier to hunt. If a buck feeds at such and such a place each evening, the hunter just has to wait somewhere along his feeding trail to collect him. (Of course, it's never quite that easy; nothing in hunting is.)

Despite the differences in temperament, there are quite a lot of similarities in behavior between mule and white-tailed deer. They both rut at about the same time, though the whitetails' rut is more intense and generally shorter lived. Mule deer may begin rutting in earnest early in November—I've found the peak of rutting activity of three herds I studied in three western states to fall somewhere between November 11 and 22—and may rut longer into December than whitetails. I'm told by several guides and outfitters in Alberta and Saskatchewan that the whitetail peak of rutting activity can be predicted almost to the day. Two Alberta guides told me that rutting peaks were on November 18 and 19. A Saskatchewan guide and an outfitter told me rutting peaks in the central part of the province near Marsh Lake were always between November 17 and 19. Mule deer, on the other hand, are not that predictable; I've found rutting peaks of one particular herd in the Wasatch Mountains of northeastern Utah to vary from November 12 to 26 in two consecutive years. Since a whitetail ruts more intensely within a shorter period of time, he's more apt to make mistakes during the rut than a muley, which ruts less intensely over a longer period of time.

With the numbers of hunters afield these days, whitetail and muley bucks alike take to the timber and brush during daylight hours. Still hunting and stalking in timber are the same for whitetails as for mule deer, and both require caution and patience. (For more details, see chapter 5.) A whitetail buck also has a home range and a center, or core, area. The whitetail inhabits it for a greater part of the year than does a mule deer and is more territorial. As such, the whitetail is less likely to leave its home range because of disturbance during hunting seasons, so a hunter is apt to find the buck in that same area even if he's already missed a chance at it. A mule deer migrates vertically and may have as many as six home ranges in a given year; it's also more likely to leave the area if frightened by a hunter.

Mule deer and whitetail tracks are about the same size, though whitetail tracks seem to be a tad slimmer and more streamlined than those of muleys. I haven't gotten a caliper to confirm it, but this might be because mule deer generally inhabit rougher and rockier country, so their hooves have become worn and rounded by contact with rocks and gravel. You can track a whitetail buck just as you can a mule deer, and like muleys, big whitetail bucks tend to bed downwind and within sight of their backtrails. Whitetails are affected by weather just as mule deer are, and they tend to bed in similar "safe" places.

I believe that there are more truly fanatic whitetail hunters than mule deer hunters, and there's even a magazine just for whitetail hunters. There are any number of whitetail hunting clubs scattered throughout the country, and whitetail hunters in general seem to be a more knowledgeable lot than mule deer, elk, or pronghorn hunters. A higher proportion of whitetail hunters can identify the track of a big buck, rattle, use vocal calls, wear appropriate hunting garb, use biology to bag bucks, and are aware of artificial and natural masking and luring scents.

The two main behavioral differences of whitetails—their persistence in keeping or reestablishing routines and their flighty, nervous nature—are really the chinks in their armor. That's not to say that man-wise veteran whitetails don't make some pretty smart and incredibly effective escape maneuvers, however. But a whitetail is easier to drive than a big mule deer buck because he's more predictable and nervous. And it's easier to ambush a good whitetail buck as he makes the rounds of his scrape line or leaves the meadow where he feeds along the same trail he always uses. Driving and ambushing are the only methods used by many Canadian guides. It's easier to find the center area of a whitetail buck's home range, because chances are he's been there longer than a mule deer would have been and there are more tracks, rubs, scrapes, beds, droppings, and other sign. It's also easier to approach this center area because the whitetail buck has been there longer without disturbance and he's more secure there and more likely to let his guard down a little than a mule deer would be.

I once walked into a whitetail buck's center area and jumped him from his bed at twenty yards simply by following a well-used trail that led from a big alfalfa field into a tangle of willows. I wasn't particularly quiet, and the buck apparently had never been bothered there before and didn't expect it. The buck nearly had a fit trying to get out of the tangle, and I'm sure I could have collected him had I been so inclined. My longtime hunting buddy Rick Lovell once walked right into a whitetail's center area without the buck's suspecting a thing. Rick and the buck saw each other at about the same time from perhaps twenty yards, and the buck nearly trampled Rick trying to escape. Rick stuck a .30/.30 slug through the buck's lungs, and he had his biggest whitetail ever. That doesn't often happen these days with trophy mule deer, though, at least not with those that have been hunted before (and most have).

It's also much easier to rattle in a whitetail than a mule deer. In fact, most hunters don't know it's even possible to rattle in mule deer at all (it is, but only under certain conditions). Rattling for whitetails works best just before the rut. It does work during the peak of the rut, but not as well, and the bucks that respond then tend to be younger animals rather than trophies. On my first attempt at rattling in central Saskatchewan, I brought in a fair 8-pointer. I didn't shoot because I was after a big one that was in the area, but that smaller buck wouldn't leave until I climbed down out of the tree stand.

Just before the peak of the rut, bucks are wandering around their home ranges trying to determine who the competition is. They determine this by sparring—putting their antlers together and shoving to test each other's strength. This avoids serious, potentially fatal battles later on during the rut, which usually only happen when two strangers of equal size and strength meet. Since bucks are trying to find out who they can beat and what their place in the hierarchy is, they're attracted to the clatter of antlers in the woods.

When rattling, it's best to clatter the antlers together lightly at first. If you do it too loudly at close range—and you can never tell if there's a buck hiding in a thicket within a few yards of your tree stand—you're apt to frighten a buck off. If no buck answers this initial rattling, try it a bit louder. If it's windy or there's other noise, you'll also need to rattle a little louder.

All members of the deer family are attracted to rattling or clattering antlers at some time during the breeding season, some more so than others. Though whitetails, and perhaps moose, respond best, mule deer and elk will also come in when the situation is just right. Why whitetails are more easily rattled than mule deer is anyone's guess. I've heard several biological theories, but none sounds too convincing to me.

White-tailed deer are a midsuccessional species, as are elk, moose, and mule deer. This means that they are attracted to openings where plant succession hasn't reached the climax, or heavy forest, stage. They feed on shrubs, forbs, and grasses that grow in such openings and on farmers' crops such as wheat, alfalfa, and oats. They're able to make a living in eastern hardwood forests by feeding on mast such as acorns and beechnuts. They prefer bedding in heavy cover, broken by meadows, old burns, and other clearings. So, ideally, the best whitetail habitat is a region with forests and swamps for bedding and escape cover and also with meadows, burns, and agricultural fields for feed. I've hunted just that type of country in Canada, and it was noted for huge bucks. Unfortunately, I have yet to get one or even see one on the hoof, but I have seen their tracks, mounted heads, and even a few dead animals bagged by luckier hunters.

While some very large deer are coming out of the broken woods-and-farmlands country of Alberta and Saskatchewan, hunters are also continuing to take huge bucks from large south Texas ranches and adjacent Mexico. Texas bucks tend to be smaller in body size and have thinner antlers than their Canadian cousins, but since they are smaller, the big antlers look positively gargantuan. There have been many record-class heads harvested from south Texas ranches, and since whitetails represent an important cash source for ranchers (hunts on the best are going for about five grand these days), the deer herds are scientifically managed, culled, and even fed — which then raises the question of whether they're truly wild.

In southern Arizona there's a tiny subspecies of whitetail known as the Coues deer. In much of its range it behaves very similarly to mule deer, and like them, it inhabits steep, rocky, and semiopen mountainsides and canyons. Hunting them can be more like hunting mule deer, or even mountain sheep, than like hunting whitetails in eastern hardwoods or Canadian farmlands. A hunter will often locate the Coues deer from a distance by glassing, and then plan and execute a sneak. The animal is frequently shot as it makes its escape across a canyon or ravine. It's tough to get a Coues whitetail permit these days, however, since they're available only by drawing. Probably the best places to hunt these deer include the mountains north and west of Nogales, the Chiricahuas, and perhaps the Huachucas, all in Arizona.

My very first deer was a nice, 8-point Coues deer buck I bagged in the mountains near Patagonia, Arizona, not far from the Mexican border, back when I was thirteen or so. It would have made the record book, but over the years, with all of my moves and traveling, I've lost the antlers. I shot the deer late in the evening in an arroyo thick with mesquite and acacia, and I was never more thrilled with a deer.

10

The Adaptable
and Cunning Leopard

Professional hunter John A. Hunter wrote a book in 1952 about his experiences in East Africa. It quickly became a big seller in the United States and much of the English-speaking world. In *Hunter*, he tells of his adventures as a professional hunter for some of the world's wealthiest clients and about his game-control work for the government. Very few people, including the hunter-explorers of the last century, have even approached the type of experience that Hunter has. Hunter did not write in hyperbole, so he gives the sense that what he says can be believed.

In his work, Hunter killed hundreds, perhaps thousands, of rhinos, elephants, lions, buffalo, and leopards, mostly in order to make portions of East Africa safe for its increasing populations. From his vast experience, Hunter believes the leopard to be Africa's most dangerous game. He considers the elephant the least dangerous, because it seldom charges unprovoked, is large and slow and thus easy to shoot, and will turn from a charge if hit. The rhino is a bit more dangerous because it frequently charges with little or no provocation. The lion and buffalo are next—they're smaller targets, relatively fast, and more determined when they do charge. The leopard is an even smaller target and is quicker by far than any of the others. It doesn't give its presence away with a warning growl, and short of your blasting the animal to pieces, if it is charging, it will not be stopped. To quote John Hunter: "All in all, I know of no beast I would less wish to hunt in cover than the fast, savage, cunning leopard."

In Africa the leopard ranges from the dry, suffocating, blistering deserts in the extreme south to the dripping equatorial jungles and northward. It is found in the Indian subcontinent, northward through the Himalayas and into China, eastward through the Indochina peninsula, and even as far north as Mongolia. It lives in diverse habitats, from steaming lowland rain forests to the highest mountain peaks. It can tolerate the 135° heat of the Kalahari Desert or the below-zero temperatures and heavy snows in the high mountain ranges of Asia. In the prologue to *The Snows of Kilimanjaro*, Ernest Hemingway tells of the dried and frozen carcass of a leopard near the summit of that mountain at nearly twenty thousand feet.

The leopard is a highly adaptable animal and, in a time when species are disappearing every day, continues to live contentedly on, shifting its diet when people move to its territory from game to dogs, barnyard fowl, livestock, rats, lizards, snakes, or garbage, and once in a while, it even snatches a human. In colonial India the Rudraprayag Maneater accounted for 126 confirmed human kills over eight years, although most experts believe the actual tally to be at least twice that. The famous Jim Corbett, after years of hunting him and probably some close calls, finally killed the old male leopard by sitting up for him with a flashlight at night. In some parts of rural Africa today, children and even women are still sometimes snatched from villages.

The leopard has highly acute vision and hearing but a relatively poor sense of smell compared with that of deer, antelope, or bears. Though this is unusual for a forest or savanna animal, it is characteristic of the cat family, Felidae. By the restricted definition of stalking—that is, it begins only after game is sighted—the leopard is seldom stalked. By the broad definition, which includes still hunting and tracking, even sneaking up on known leopard cover, the big cat is sometimes stalked.

The classic—and favorite—method of bagging a leopard these days is baiting. In my experience, there are few things as adrenaline-pumping as baiting for leopards. Often it's necessary for the client and his professional hunter (PH) to stalk the blind before hiding in it and to get into it as quietly as possible. Frequently the leopard is hiding close by, at least within earshot, and knows there are humans nearby. One ploy is to have some humans approach the bait, then some leave again, with two remaining behind in the blind. This often fools the leopard into thinking they've all gone. Sometimes he'll play it safe, though, and investigate the blind closely before showing himself, even in the dark.

For years leopard baiting has been done during the evening hours just before dark. But as I said, the leopard is an adaptable animal. Those cats that show themselves at baits before dark are being killed off. The smarter cats, those that refuse to show up until after dark, are the ones that are surviving and breeding, and intelligent and nocturnal mothers are teaching this behavior to their kittens. I wouldn't be surprised if within a decade or so all leopards in hunted country will only feed at baits at night. That's the way it already is in much of Zimbabwe and the Republic of South Africa today.

Most of Zimbabwe (formerly Rhodesia) is ranch country, and predators are not looked upon kindly. Lions and hyenas have long since been exterminated in these parts, as have fence-destroying and sometimes cattle-killing elephants, rhinos, and buffalo. This is permitted because game on private lands is considered the property of the rancher. These days, however, it seems that more and more ranchers have through frustration given up trying to exterminate the crafty leopard and have learned to live with it. Many have made the cat pay its way: The landowner collects a trophy fee, which, for a leopard in Zimbabwe these days, starts at fifteen hundred U.S. dollars. In addition, there's a daily hunting fee of four hundred to twelve hundred dollars, which goes to the landowner or safari operator. If the land belongs to a local community cooperative, the usually very poor rural farmers living there get the money. If the land is federal, the government gets the trophy fees. Hunting leopards has turned into a big, profitable business.

And there are an astounding number of leopards. I hunted both in western Zimbabwe and in the extreme south, and in both places leopard spoor, or sign, which includes tracks, droppings, and other signs of passage, was virtually everywhere. We couldn't go out hunting a day, whether we were after sable, kudu, or wildebeest without running across fresh tracks or even a kill drag mark in the sand. A walking leopard's hind foot steps on the forepaw print. If it's trotting, the hindpaw print is a bit ahead of the forepaw print—just like deer in North America.

Once we even saw a leopard lying on a kopje, or small hill, in broad daylight. His head was visible above the rocks at two hundred yards. Normally I might have taken the shot—I had often shot ground squirrels out to three hundred yards and was consistent on them at

My first leopard bagged in Zimbabwe. It measured 7 feet 2 inches from nose to tail.
Cheri Flory.

two hundred. I declined this shot, however, partly because only a small portion of the cat's exposed head would be a fatal zone, while a hit somewhere else would allow the animal to crawl off and die miserably, perhaps starving to death with a broken jaw or severed jaw muscles. Another consideration was that I would have to pay the fifteen-hundred-dollar trophy fee even if I just nicked the animal, and I wasn't solvent enough to afford that.

We pulled off a classic sneak on the kopje anyway, circling downwind to the back of the boulder hill and approaching laboriously through the mopane scrub. Trackers Shorty and Luka led, I followed, and professional hunter Russell Tarr and Cheri brought up the rear. There were big tracks in the sand, and plenty of them, which indicated that the big leopard was using the kopje regularly. But we didn't find the cat, although we scoured the area, nor could we find where he'd left the kopje. We had seen that leopard while on the way to the blind where I would kill another big cat later that night.

Our very first night in the "hide," as they call it in Africa, we'd waited for a big male that had been feeding on half a donkey tied to a stout sausage tree. The tracks were big—larger and, to my eye, more blocky than the prints made by a female, and they were pressed deeply into the soil. The outsized cat would have made an excellent trophy. He didn't feed on the bait every night; adult males feed only a little at a time and often several days apart. When he did visit the bait, he came off an immense kopje half overgrown with trees and thick brush. He would either move directly to the bait or hit the Land Rover track and walk down it to the bait. We sat in the blind that night, a flimsy affair of burlap and grass, and I recalled John Hunter's thoughts on the danger of hunting leopards. I shivered in the June cold as jackals wailed out of the darkness, sounding nearly like Utah coyotes, and owls and other night birds called and echoed from the immense, black boulder hills.

From what I'd read, leopards came to the baits in the early evening, and concealed clients picked a rosette just over a cat's heart through the rifle scope and potted the animal out of the tree at forty yards. Not so here; this was cattle country, and leopards had been heavily persecuted for well over a century. Those that survived were "supercats"—the brainiest of an already intelligent animal. A leopard here wouldn't show himself until well after dark. Those that had come out early had long since been shot off.

It was planned that, when the cat got well into its eating in the darkness, Russell would flip on the spotlight after I'd eased the gun into the blind opening, hoping the trophy would stay just long enough for me to get a bullet into a vital place. Cheri was along for the thrill. June in the Southern Hemisphere is winter, and by dark we were shivering beneath four layers of clothing. I understood the odds were all in favor of the leopard. Russell told me about a client who had spent eighteen afternoon-to-dawn vigils in a blind. At least this kind of hunting wasn't as bad as running the animals down in cars across an open desert, as was routinely practiced by the largest safari company in Botswana, or trapping them in steel-jaw traps on a bait and taking the client to the crazed animal (as practiced by a well-known ranch-hunt operator in Namibia). (My friend Jack Brusatori told me of one such "hunt" with one of the biggest outfitters near Mt. Etjo. "I'll never do it again" was how he ended his narrative.)

Several hours after dark, when the cold had penetrated into my bones and hung on like a pit bull with lockjaw, I heard something just outside the hide. Immediately all the cold was gone, and my heart was in my throat and pounding so loudly I was sure anything out there could hear it. The tension from Russell and Cheri was palpable. Something was walking toward the bait across the dried leaves on my side of the blind. I fingered the rifle, getting ready to slip it into the opening. Russell gripped my arm—our prearranged signal—then released it, and I eased the .270 into position. Russell flicked on the light and something—definitely not a leopard, though—darted away. "Bushpig," Russell whispered in my ear. I had no feeling of cold for the rest of the night, and I doubt my pulse returned to within ten beats of normal until we were back at camp.

I could hardly wait to get into the blind the next afternoon. While we sat in the hide, we heard the animal sounds change with the passing of the day—from the monotonous buzzing of blowflies and the croaks of hornbills feeding on maggots on the bait when we arrived, to the calls of strange birds somewhere beyond the immense kopje at dusk, and then to the faint whistlings of tiny owls and the occasional wail of a jackal in the darkness. I was mesmerized and absorbed in the African night sounds when, without warning, there came a sound that made us all jump.

In this part of Africa it's called "coughing," and in others, "sawing." Neither name comes close to describing the deep, rasping, rumbling growl that at close range you can feel vibrating through the air and earth, into your feet and skin, and up your bones to your heart and soul. No other sound does the same things to your guts. And though I'd never heard it close up before, there was no mistaking it now.

The tension in the blind was so thick it was almost suffocating, and Russell's hand trembled as he gripped my forearm. His breathing was short and rapid. I guess no matter how many times you've hunted leopards, you never get used to that first cough. Then the big cat coughed again, this time from farther up the kopje. He knew we were there and he was mad about it. We all knew he wouldn't come again that night, though we stayed in the hide, hoping against the odds that he would, until Luka returned with the Land Rover.

"I heard him behind us," Cheri said as we unfolded our cold and tension-stiff frames from the blind. Russell and I had heard nothing, though I'd sensed something in the darkness at my back—something that made the hairs on my neck stand on end. Cheri's hearing was better than mine—she hadn't fired too many big guns like I had—and then for proof there were saucer-sized pug marks five yards from where we had sat behind a flimsy cover of burlap and grass. It crossed my mind that we were hunting leopards just as Jim Corbett had done and just as he had finally killed the Rudraprayag Maneater.

"You can't beat it," I was thinking aloud as the Rover rattled for camp and a black-and-white civet bounded out of the darkness and back again.

"You can't until a bloody spotted bush-puss jumps into the hide with you," Russell chuckled.

Sitting in the blind that night had given me more gut-twisting, adrenaline-pumping excitement than had hunting all the sable, kudu, reedbuck, and wildebeest we'd already bagged combined. That night alone was worth the price of the safari.

The next day we traveled south to another camp on a tributary of the Limpopo River for waterbuck and bushbuck. Meanwhile, Pierre, an apprentice PH, had been putting out leopard baits. When we arrived in camp, Pierre told us that clients had pulled out of a leopard blind at seven the evening before—much too early—in order to travel to another camp and hunt tsessebe. Upon dismantling the blind that day, Pierre noticed the spoor of a male and a female leopard that had fed on the impala baits. Russell said it sounded too good to be true, so we rushed back and rebuilt the blind.

Just before dark a civet trotted up a sloping tree to the baits and began to feed. Later, closer to dark, a honey badger began to eat, standing on his hind legs and reaching for a dangling impala leg. His claws scratching against the bark in the darkness kept me fingering the rifle. The badger fed noisily for an hour, then it was suddenly quiet. I knew from the thick silence that the leopard was there. If there had been any doubt, the spotted cat started a deep, constant, rumbling, purring growl. It was unlike the cough we had heard at the other blind, but it, too, vibrated through the air and ground and into my guts. I was strangely calm, however; the loud-feeding honey badger and the initial adrenaline rush from the leopard's first presence had drained the excitement away, and I was ready for whatever was next.

With hand pressure, Russell made me understand that it wasn't time—the leopard was not feeding yet. Then the purring growl moved off, and I felt sure that it was over and the cat was leaving. But then the sound came back again, closer now, and I could again feel it inside of me. At times I felt as if the deep purring surrounded me, or that there were two leopards. Then it was quiet again. Russell's hand was on my arm a moment after I heard the faint crunching and slurping as the cat went to work on the impala, and he held my arm for what seemed eons.

I'd rehearsed it all in my mind, and I slid automatically to the .270 perched in the blind opening, my eye instinctively lining up with the scope even though I could see nothing. Then the impalas hung in the trees were illuminated, but there was no leopard, no movement. I eased the scope to the edge of the opening and back again. Still nothing. Then a big, spotted head came up out of the high grass, nose in the air and chewing, incredibly still oblivious. I moved the cross hairs to the base of his neck without conscious thought, and my finger tightened on the trigger. I did not feel the recoil and I don't remember the muzzle flash. There was no sign of the cat.

Russell hadn't seen the leopard, though he had seen some movement out from the bait. "Are you sure it wasn't a jackal?" he asked.

I answered that it was a leopard, preoccupied with watching through the scope in case the cat, invisible now in the grass, showed itself.

"You're sure you didn't shoot a jackal?"

"It was a leopard," I told him again, still looking through the rifle scope.

"You're sure?" he asked again. I didn't answer.

Earlier we'd agreed that Russell would approach any downed leopard alone. At first I'd insisted on going, too, but that would perhaps compromise Russell some since, as a professional hunter, he'd have to worry about a client's safety as well as the leopard. I unfortunately understood the logic. So I covered Russell as he approached the bait, the cross hairs solid on the place where the leopard had disappeared. Through the scope, I watched as Russell tossed a stick into the grass, then another, and finally approached and lifted a big, spotted paw so I could see it. "Big damn jackal," I deadpanned after

Cheri and I had walked over to the cat, all seven feet, four inches of it stretched out on the grass.

Luka and Shorty had heard the shot and they drove up in the Land Rover. They shook my hand and pulled my thumb respectfully and jubilantly. It was all very jolly, and I'd never experienced anything quite like it.

On the drive back to camp Russell leaned on the "tooter" almost continuously, often hooting himself, and once there made a turn through camp and then drove out to the game pole, honking all the while. The entire camp staff turned out, and we took photos by head-lights and spotlight. This was something special, more momentous than the big antelope we'd been bringing in. Luka pulled a fist-sized chunk of impala meat from the cat's jaws. The leopard had died instantly, had felt nothing, and that was important to me.

That leopard hunt was one of my most exciting hunts ever. If I hunt leopards again, I'll again do it by baiting, although there are other methods. In several places in southern Africa, but mostly in the Kalahari Desert, leopards are tracked across vast plains for days on end by experienced and gifted trackers, mostly Bushman, and the PH and client follow in a hunting car. When the cat can or will go no farther, he makes his stand and is usually shot from the car. There's an elevated seat and platform in the back that makes this easy. I've watched several videos of this kind of shooting, and there seems little sport and little danger in killing leopards this way, though I know of one Botswana PH who was mauled when a leopard jumped into the car.

I once met an out-of-work PH in Riley's Bar in Maun, Botswana, who had located leopards on immense islands in the Okavango Delta by their spoor, then stalked the cat's cover. Though the cats had always escaped to adjacent islands, he thought they could be taken that way with a little practice. Jim Corbett also mentions tracking and stalking leopards to their lairs in the jungles of northern India; he considered it great fun to get a photo of one this way. Most European and American clients in Africa have had no practice at moving quietly through the bush, however, and I doubt that stalking and tracking leopards is really a possibility for them.

Willie Phillips, a gifted Botswana professional hunter, told me he'd seen several obviously pregnant female leopards shot in the Kala-hari Desert after they'd been trailed by hunting cars. With practices like these, it's no wonder there's so much antihunting sentiment these days.

In spite of safari company abuses, though, I've seen a great deal of leopard spoor in several spots in Botswana and all over Zimbabwe, and a friend who recently got back from Zambia said leopard sign was "all over the place." Another sportsman who'd just made a successful safari to Mozambique for lions and buffalo told me the leopards were so numerous they'd jumped into the hunting car for some game meat while the hunters were out tracking some beast or other. He'd also seen the big cats walking along the tracks in daylight. In 1989, when he'd hunted there, leopards were protected.

Russell Tarr told us one evening of some tricks Republic of South Africa professional hunters of his acquaintance had used. One of them had been caught at it the year before. That PH had purchased several leopards from a game farm and, while they were caged, shot them through the ear with a .22 so there'd be no apparent bullet hole. The entire leopard was then frozen and hidden in a tree over the bait. The innovative PH would put his client in the blind and, after a suitable length of time, direct his spotlight at just the right angle to show the leopard. The client would shoot, the PH's accomplice would pull a rope, and the leopard would topple from the tree. The PH would tell the client that the cat was only wounded and they'd come back for it in the morning. By then, of course, the leopard would be thawed and the client none the wiser. One client, however, was not to be put off. He insisted on looking for the animal then and there and found the frozen leopard. The PH's gig was up and he lost his license. The fact that there are so many unfair and shady methods of bagging a leopard indicates the difficulty of collecting the animal fairly.

Russell admitted that his mother has shot more leopards than he will ever get. When he was young, his family members were stationed throughout southern Africa in the military. Leopards frequently would raid livestock in neighboring villages. Since his father was away much of the time and his mother had the only gun, she'd be called upon to dispatch the marauding leopards, often when they were still at work in corrals or bomas. Russell said his mother shot some very good ones, too.

Russell felt that the leopard and buffalo are Africa's most dangerous game, and he'd hunted all but the rhino, which is about impossible to shoot these days except on South African ranches at exorbitant trophy fees. If you're rich enough to afford it, it's a bit like shooting a cow in a pasture.

For the time being, leopard populations, especially in southern Africa, seem remarkably healthy and vigorous, and hunting them there should remain an attractive sport, especially if some abusive practices can be curtailed. I've killed probably twenty head of African game, and I value leopard right up there with buffalo trophies.

11

Stalking
the Cape Buffalo

The Cape buffalo can be found from the desert fringes of the Kalahari in Botswana and the Republic of South Africa to the forests of central Africa and the savanna country of East Africa. Savannas seem to be the typical habitat of the Cape buffalo, and the typical herd feeds in the open at night and in the morning and evening and retires to heavy brush or trees during the day. The harder a local population of buffalo is hunted, the more nocturnal they tend to be. In more than a few places, these great, scaly, black wild oxen only feed out of the timber in darkness.

Cape buffalo are frequently stalked by still hunting, tracking, or ambushing. Another method often used these days is to drive around in a Land Rover or Toyota truck (the two most common vehicles in Africa), spot a herd, and sneak up on it. Sometimes fresh tracks are found and the hunters trail the herd, which is about as difficult as trailing half a dozen D-9 Cats. Sneaking up close to a Cape buffalo isn't easy, however. All of the buffalo's senses are equally well developed. They see better than any of the other wild cattle and than most antelope. Their sense of smell is better than that of the big cats and probably than that of the most common antelope, and they trust their sense of smell more, too. They also have incredible hearing.

When pulling off a sneak on a herd of buffalo, it's necessary to stay completely out of sight and to keep downwind. Be sure to approach pretty directly into the wind so that any buffalo spread out from the herd won't scent you as they might if the wind were drifting from the side. Being quiet isn't quite as important, since the herd makes a considerable din as the animals chew, grunt, gurgle, low, and force their way through thornbush. It *is* important, though, not to make a distinctly odd noise such as squeaking your sling swivel, scraping stiff fabric against brush, or clinking cartridges together.

Everyone with experience in the African bush agrees that the Cape buffalo is one of Africa's most dangerous animals. Many think it is *the* most dangerous. Late nineteenth-century explorer and hunter Frederick C. Selous had several close encounters with buffalo. Once he was charged by a cow shot through both lungs with a four-bore he used on elephants. (That's with a lead ball having, if my calculations are correct, a weight of four ounces!) He had another close call when a bull charged him as he chased it on horseback. The buffalo hit the horse, disemboweling it and sending the horse, Selous, and the gun in different directions. Incredibly, Selous escaped that one too. Selous also listed in his book *A Hunter's Wanderings in Africa* a number of friends and acquaintances who had had very close encounters with buffalo; some of them survived and some did not.

Professional hunter J. A. Hunter, whom I discussed in chapter 10, considered the Cape buffalo very dangerous indeed. According to Hunter, the buffalo would charge unprovoked, as determinedly as they come, and with "admirable ferocity," and it would not flinch away from a bullet. Hunter continues on the dangers of buffalo hunting: "I consider the heaviest rifle a man can conveniently carry none too powerful for buffalo." Hunter tells of several incidents where natives had been worked over by buffalo. One native honey gatherer was castrated by a charging bull he'd surprised and was thoroughly pummeled before the bull left him for dead. The native finally came to his senses, broken, battered, and weak from loss of blood. He lay in the open bush for two weeks eating grass before other honey gatherers found him and carried him to the village.

Hunter lost his close personal friend, right-hand man, gunbearer, and tracker, Kirakangano, to a big buffalo bull that had been wounded by a prince he declines to name. Hunter notes that the prince was afraid of big guns and went after the buffalo with a rifle too light for the job. He gut-shot a bull that made it into heavy cover, and Kirakangano spoored it down and pointed it out standing in brush for an ambush. The bull realized he'd been spotted and whirled off into cover. They repeated that performance several times until the affair began to tell on the prince's nerves, who insisted on being taken back out of the thick brush. Hunter had no choice but to obey. He left Kirakangano and the prince's inexperienced but arrogant gunbearer with orders not to follow the bull farther.

The prince's gunbearer took matters into his own hand and went after the buffalo, which predictably charged. The gunbearer ran back toward Kirakangano, hoping the bull would shift his attentions to the other man. As the prince's man came abreast of Kirakangano, the bull caught the gunbearer and catapulted him ahead, breaking his neck in two places. The bull then worked over Kirakangano, who'd been armed only with a spear. Hunter had heard the pounding and grunting of the furious bull goring Kirakangano. Kirakangano was a frightful mess when Hunter returned and killed the bull. There was a smile on Kirakangano's face when he heard that the prince's man was dead. Kirakangano, also, died of his wounds.

In Botswana, professional hunter Willie Phillips, six Bushman and Bayei trackers and skinners, Cheri, and I sneaked into the midst of about forty buffalo, where I shot a good bull through the heart at fifteen yards. We had cover along almost the entire route of the sneak, and we kept downwind. With that many people, it was impossible to keep absolutely quiet, but we did move without any undue noise, and apparently the buffalo were making enough of their own that they didn't hear us.

Earlier on that hunt we had found buffalo spoor and spent the better part of a day following it. We did get close to a dozen or so bulls, but none was worth shooting. Once a Bayei, Bushman, or Matabele tracker picks up spoor, you can safely wager six months' salary that you'll catch sight of game. At least that's been my experience.

The day I shot my bull on one of the immense islands of the Okavango Delta in Botswana, we'd started a sneak on an arm of a big herd grazing in high grass in the late morning. The sneak had worked perfectly, the palm and acacia cover and the wind had been just right, and we'd been able to move into the wind from clump to clump of palms until we were very close. We were so close I could hear their bellies gurgling and smell the sweet, cowy, barnyard fragrance. Willie eased through some palms on a tussock and motioned for me to follow. I did so, my heart pounding loudly in my ears. I was way too excited, and oddly, as I peeked through the palms at a bull only twenty yards away, I kept remembering some of the more gruesome hunter-buffalo encounters I'd read about over the years.

For a moment I thought I would faint as the bull profiled briefly and Willie motioned me to be ready. My heart was still pounding when the bull turned his backside toward us and walked off into the herd. Willie wasn't sure of my abilities with a rifle at that time, and he wisely didn't permit me to shoot the bull in that position. Unfortunately the big bull disappeared in the high grass without offering a safe shot. In a way, that was a good encounter for me to have, since it cleared away my nervousness; when I finally did shoot a bull late in the hunt, I was as cool as a Yukon toilet seat.

A bit later we located another part of the herd feeding in the open. The wind would be just right if we circled a bit to get it more directly in our faces, and there seemed to be enough palm and acacia cover to approach from that direction. We eased through the grass and often knee-deep water, using the small islets of palms for cover. About midway in the sneak, we came across several warthogs rooting about in the dust of a high piece of ground. Willie motioned me to shoot the one nearest. I protested that I didn't want to spook the buffalo, since they were only four hundred yards away.

"It's a good warthog," Willie said in that cool, calming way he has that's calculated to reduce the adrenaline level in a client.

"But I don't want to spook the buffalo," I hissed back while looking anxiously their way.

"Bugger the buffalo, shoot the bloody warthog!" Willie had momentarily lost his cool. Joseph, the Bayei tracker, jammed a thick forked stick into the mud so I could shoot standing to clear the high grass, and I rested the fore end of the .270 in the fork. I still didn't want to shoot and was a bit put out that Willie was insisting I shoot a lousy warthog when we were close to sticking distance on the buffalo. Willie knew buffalo was my number one priority on this hunt. I pressed the trigger and took the slack out. The gun roared and kicked, and there was a puff of dust on the hog's shoulder. He turned and trotted for cover, and I heard the rumble of the big buffalo herd like distant thunder over the swamp as they stampeded for cover.

I looked at Willie as if to say "I told you so!" as the rumbling herd departed and a great cloud of dust rose from the acacia trees. Willie looked toward where the warthog had disappeared in the low palms and said, "Dead."

And it was. The warthog had made it to his burrow and was just backing in when it died; the bullet had passed through its heart. Willie, not normally an excitable chap when after game, was as excited as I'd ever seen him. He gripped my hand in a hard and heartfelt handshake and mentioned something about that being a *real* trophy, as if everything else we'd collected were nothings. With the other kills, he'd merely given a thumbs up sign for congratulations. I knew next to nothing about warthogs, and was unimpressed when he measured the tusks at twelve inches where they entered the gum. When removed, they measured at more than fifteen inches, and that, hunters, is a huge warthog. It would have been in the top ten of the SCI records if I had chosen to list it, although I didn't. The tusks were also exceptionally heavy. That's beginner's luck!

We picked up the buffalo tracks and started to follow again. The tracks spread over a front a quarter mile wide, and they were moving into the wind. We were all sneaking as quietly as safari ants on the sand, occasionally stopping to unhook a "wait-a-bit" thorn from clothing or an ear. Before long we were jumping small groups of buffalo from either side, and several times we had forty of the creatures stampeding on both sides and within thirty yards or so. Other times we'd round a clump of acacia scrub and come face-to-face with bulls glaring at us as if we'd insulted their politics. The bulls would whip their tails, whirl, and gallop off into the bush. I supposed we were

My first Cape buffalo, killed in the Okavango Delta of Botswana. Professional hunter Willie Phillips is on the right. *Cheri Flory.*

following specific tracks, but I had neither time nor opportunity to ask. I whispered to Cheri to always keep a tree in mind for climbing should the need arise. We were in close to buffalo almost every minute on that trail.

As we trotted around the bleached carcasses of acacia trees that had been pulled down by elephants, we skidded to a stop as an immense bull stood broadside glaring suspiciously. Willie motioned me forward so I could shoot through a screen of thornbush, but the bull whirled and lumbered off, followed by his entourage of mature bulls. "Forty-five bloody inches!" Willie muttered.

We kept going, seldom slackening the pace, until late in the evening as the sun slanted into the northwest, when we found a herd grazing placidly at the far end of a grassy meadow near a small water hole. We circled quickly to a tangle of palms four hundred yards downwind for cover, then circled more to get the wind more directly into our faces so there'd be no possibility of an outrider bull scenting us. The herd was completely out of sight as we stalked through the palms and acacia. I'd lost track of the buffalo as we sloshed as quietly as possible through ankle-deep water toward a small, palm-covered island. Once we were on it, Willie motioned for Cheri to get close and then crept ahead. When he parted some palms, the buffalo were there—practically in our laps!

"When he turns broadside, take the nearest bull," Willie whispered to me calmly in the same tone of voice he'd use to ask someone to pass the dessert, as if this were the most common thing in the world and he did it every day.

The bull was fifteen yards away, and as he turned broadside, I touched the set trigger. The rifle went off, sounding more like a firecracker than a .375, and the herd milled for a moment in confusion and then galloped off. I jumped clear of the palms to get a better shot at the bull as it lumbered by, and Willie hissed, "Don't move, don't move!" but a bit too late. I was lucky, and the buffalo didn't whirl and charge; I had time for a second shot at the bull at ten yards, and I actually saw the bullet hit and the sudden, white hole in the scaly, dark hide just where the heart should be as the bull kept going, blood exploding now in great glouts from his nostrils. I knew he was dead, but I hit him again as he quartered away at a hundred yards just before he entered thick bush cover, and suddenly he was down and the trackers and skinners were shouting and cheering.

Joseph said something to me in Tswana, then shook my hand and pulled my thumb in congratulations. "He says, 'Today you shoot like a man,'" Willie explained. Apparently, he was ribbing me about a rather poor showing on a red lechwe the day before. I guess the buffalo and the one-shot kill on the warthog made up for it. Willie shook my hand again fiercely; twice in one day, and the only times on the entire safari. Triumph is so sweet.

The bull I had collected was a prime herd bull with a spread just over 40 inches and with 14-inch bosses that came together solidly. He had deep and extensive hooks that weren't worn a bit. He was more heavily furred than any buffalo I'd seen, and the hairs on his face were a very deep golden chestnut in the right light.

Award-winning taxidermist and co-owner of Atcheson Taxidermy of Butte, Montana, Tom Hardesty mounted my buff, and he's without a doubt the best looking of any of the several hundred Cape buffalo mounts I've seen over the years. Hardesty did such a good job that you can see the veins in the bull's face and the wrinkles around his eyes, ears, and neck.

Still hunting—that is, moving quietly and slowly through brush searching for whatever is there before it finds you—is another common and satisfying method of stalking buffalo. And if big and fresh buffalo tracks are found while still hunting, they're followed. We used the technique several times on our hunt in the Okavango, though without luck. We did see some good waterbuck, sitatunga, and bushbuck, though, as well as two bull elephants at twenty-five yards.

Ambushing is another method Willie uses, and it works particularly well in remote parts of the Okavango Delta because buffalo there are seldom disturbed. Buffalo typically bed in heavy cover during the day, and feed in the open in the morning and evenings; if they're heavily hunted, however, they won't move into the open unless it is dark. The buffalo in the delta weren't bothered much, and they often grazed out of the acacia tangles quite early in the afternoon and usually stayed in the open late into the morning, so ambushing was an effective tactic. Willie would frequently select a clump of palms in a wide-open grassy marsh where buffalo grazed, and then wait. He told us of sitting comfortably under a palm tree for hours one morning as buffalo grazed like so many farmyard cattle within a hundred yards. His client that day killed a fine bull with a spread in the middle 40s.

After recalling my African buffalo-hunting experiences, I find it even more difficult to decide which is the most exciting and gut-wrenching animal to stalk there. I lean toward the buffalo, but the buffalo, lion, and leopard are all more exciting than any other animal I've stalked on that continent, including the sable, kudu, waterbuck, bushbuck, and a dozen others. It must be the danger that makes these animals so fun to stalk, the idea of tempting death and then skipping lightly out of its way. Even running the Colorado River's West Water Rapids on a tractor inner tube or sky-diving through a Nevada barn roof didn't pump my adrenaline levels any higher than hunting buffalo did.

12

The Greater Kudu: Africa's Mule Deer

An old Boer farmer on whose land we'd been hunting in eastern Zimbabwe told me, "The kudu is the symbol of Africa." And if I had to choose, I, too, would pick the kudu as the most appropriate symbol of Africa. Elephants, giraffes, and rhino seem like they belong in a zoo, and all but the giraffe are found on other continents. Lions and leopards, too, have been found in Asia, and the Cape buffalo has relatives there. Most other African antelopes are not nearly as distinctive as the big, spiral-horned, striped kudu. When you first see a big kudu bull walking slowly through the mopane scrub, you'll remember that moment always, and it will be something you think about when you reminisce about Africa, as you inevitably must.

After my safari in 1989 to a remote part of the Okavango Delta in Botswana, we flew out to the city of Maun over the swamps and islands of the delta. We'd had an absolutely incredible time hunting and watching wildlife with our PH, Willie Phillips. It had been a journey back in time to primeval Africa, which I had thought no longer existed, in an untouched part of the continent, so it was understandable that we felt sad as the Cessna 207 flew low over the verdant green, grassy marshes and the dry, palm-covered islands. We saw elephants, giraffes, buffalo, herds of tsessebee, red lechwe, impalas, and zebras. Several small groupings of lions glared at us as we passed low overhead, including two big, heavily maned males. One thing that surprised me, though, was that at least three times we spotted kudu bedded in the brush of small islands. Apparently they would wade through the grassy marshes, where the water was seldom deeper than knee-high to a man, to the big islands to browse. I was a bit startled because I never figured the kudu to be a swamp-dwelling animal.

In truth, kudu seldom inhabit swamps. Mostly they're found in dry country, from the Republic of South Africa through Botswana, Zimbabwe, Zambia, Namibia, and farther north to East Africa. They're not properly a desert animal, however, and do require water at times. Russell Tarr, the professional hunter on our safari in Zimbabwe, told us that numbers of kudu had died as a result of the drought in the western part of the country. People he'd known had picked up 60-inch kudu skulls. Impalas, on the other hand, had flourished during the drought and were being culled off most of the big ranches at an astounding rate. One ranch planned to cull four thousand that year.

Typically, kudu are like mule deer, elk, and Cape buffalo in their daily habits. They hole up in thick forests of scrub and feed in the savannas in the morning and evening. They're the most common and widespread of the large antelope species, and as such are the easiest to collect and the most sought after, at least in southern Africa. If you book a hunt for kudu in the Republic of South Africa, Namibia, or especially Zimbabwe, you're reasonably sure of scoring. And to me this availability doesn't make them any less desirable.

The greater part of Ernest Hemingway's nonfictional *The Green Hills of Africa* was devoted to his quest for a greater kudu trophy. Though the hunt took place in East Africa, where kudu apparently are harder to come by, Hemingway placed more value on the kudu than he did on the lions, rhino, buffalo, and other beasts he collected on that safari. His hunting party traveled to an unhunted place more than a day's journey away from base camp, where they had to hack roads through the savannas for the hunting car. After finally camping in a maize field beyond which the car couldn't go, he collected not one good bull but two in an evening. I don't believe Hemingway says at that point exactly how big the kudu were, but he mentions 52 inches somewhere later. Anything over 50 around the spiral is a good bull, and anything over 54 is excellent.

Stewart Edward White, also hunting in East Africa, writes in *Afri-*

can Campfires of his five-week quest for the kudu. According to White, "the beast is shy, it inhabits the densest, closest mountain vegetation, it possesses keen eyesight and the sense of smell of the bush-dwelling deer and antelope, and more than the average sense of hearing." The only exception I take to White's statement is his characterizing the kudu's hearing as only more than average. If you look at a kudu's ears, you'll see that they're immense. They remind me of the big, membranous ears of certain bats, and they're as big in proportion to the rest of the animal as a mule deer's ears are. In fact, hunting kudu in the savannas reminds me a great deal of hunting mule deer in much of the West: You have to be careful to stalk from downwind, you have to be very quiet and wear "quiet" clothing such as wool, and you have to keep out of sight. In places it's just like stalking mule deer in big stands of pine or fir: You must always move slowly and keep as aware as you can. The kudu's senses of hearing, sight, and smell are all fully developed and are among the best of any African game animal, though I believe that hearing is the keenest of the three.

White lucked into his kudu while walking back to camp one evening. From the photo in the book, the bull probably wouldn't tape out at much, if anything, over 40 inches. But White and his companion Cuninghame raised "a whoop of triumph" when they bagged it, and White writes, "The finest trophy in Africa was ours."

As might be expected, the kudu doesn't just stand around and let you sneak up on him. Taking a good kudu on foot is one of the greatest challenges in African hunting today. A professional hunter in Maun, Botswana, told me that the kudu killed there were rarely taken on foot; most were shot from the elevated seat in the back of a hunting car with the client resting the rifle across the cab. Kudu don't seem particularly alarmed by a hunting car, perhaps because they think of it as some big animal like a hippo. But if you're on foot and they sense you, it's another tale completely.

Several times I tried sneaking up on kudu on foot. I'd slip quietly out of the far side of the Land Rover and head for cover so I could get downwind and out of sight of the bull. It never worked. The only way I could get close to a bull on foot was to drive some distance past it and then get out as the car kept going. If the bull heard the car stop, chances are he'd take off into the *bundu*. I was always careful not to slam the door, and then I'd move back toward the bull into the wind, often having to circle to get the wind into my face. I would watch the acacia thorns scraping against my shorts or shirt, and I'd be careful not to step on any twigs that might have snapped. Then, if the bull forgot about the hunting car, if I was very careful on the stalk and didn't make a single mistake, and if I shot straight, I'd collect the bull. That's the best way to bag a kudu trophy, and you'll be more proud of it if you get it that way.

I've stalked kudu on foot a number of times, both with gun and with camera. I tried twice to get a photo of an adult bull on an expedition to Moremi Game Reserve in remote Botswana. There's no hunting on the reserve, so I was armed with only a camera. I used the breeze to my advantage, felt sure I was stalking quietly since there was no underbrush in the open forest, and tried to stay out of sight. The best photo I could manage, however, was one of the bull's south end as he headed north. I tried the following day with similar results.

The first time, I had reasoned that since we were in a place where the animals were never shot at, they'd be less wary and I'd be able to get close relatively easily. But it didn't work out that way. The second time, I planned to be more careful and sneak up on them just as if they lived in hunted country. I slid out of the Rover when it had passed half a mile down the sandy track, circled to get the wind into my face, and stalked slowly through the mopane and acacia forest. The situation seemed ideal: The bulls were still there after the car had rolled past, the forest was open with little underbrush to scrape against fabric, the ground was sandy so I could creep as quietly as a Mozambique cobra, the wind was more or less into my face, and there seemed just enough cover to keep me hidden.

Anyone who's done much wildlife photography knows that it's important to get close, even with a telephoto lens. I had a short, 210mm telephoto for my 35mm Nikon single lens reflex, so in order to get a decent picture, I'd have to be within thirty yards. I didn't really expect to get that close in view of how spooky the kudu had been, but any photo was better than none.

I eased from acacia to acacia, gradually getting nearer. Finally, after moving slowly for more than an hour, watching the wind, and taking care only to step on bare, sandy places, I saw the ivory tip of a bull's horn above the brush sixty yards away. He was looking my way, though I couldn't imagine how he'd sensed me or how and why he'd become suspicious. If he was one of the original bulls we'd spotted, there were others with him. I wondered where they were, so I scanned the brush slowly and thoroughly with binoculars. Nothing. The bull was still looking in my direction. I waited. He waited. I waited more. So did the bull. It was an impasse, but I couldn't wait all day.

Then the bull stepped toward me, curious. I remembered those immense ears; he'd probably heard some little sound I'd made. It's impossible to be absolutely silent when moving through brush, and most animals can hear sounds the human ear can't detect, so what is silent to you may be noisy to your quarry. The trick is to avoid making noises that are unnatural, such as metallic sounds or thorns scraping against stiff fabric. He stepped my way once again, moving toward an opening in the "wait-a-bit" thorn. My leg was starting to cramp, so I stepped forward maybe six inches. The bull whirled and crashed off through the scrub. I could hear other animals running off to my left. I didn't think I'd made a sound when I moved, but the bull had heard *something*.

I tried a similar stalk in Zimbabwe while trying to get close to two bulls on a kopje. We'd driven past, and I slipped out of the Rover as it moved on to fool the bulls. Then I circled the kopje. The wind was favorable, and I hoped to surprise the bulls from the other side. But I only caught a glimpse of the smaller of the two bulls running through the brush, and that was that.

I did a nearly identical sneak later in that hunt. There was a small bull standing near the top of the kopje in the open watching as the Rover motored by. A big one lay in dense thornbush. We could see the bottoms of his heavy, deeply curled horns as we idled by. He seemed to be a real trophy, so when we were out of the bulls' line of sight, I slid out of the car as it continued on, and I circled toward the bulls. I waited on the back side until Russell arrived, then we stalked silently through the open brush over the sand. The wind was good and we were quiet, and then we could see the bull still lying down. Something alerted him, though, because he stood suddenly and stared hard in our direction.

At Russell's urging, I aimed at his shoulder and touched off. The bullet punched into the flesh and bone, and a puff of dust came off as he whirled and trotted into the brush. We ran around the kopje base to head him off as he crossed the top. As he trotted under the thorn trees, I shot again. He bucked hard and trotted faster for a few yards until he collapsed. The first 150-grain .270 bullet had gone into the lungs; the second had taken him squarely through the heart. We were lucky, because there were several bulls in the area with broken horns, and we hadn't seen the tops of this bull's horns before I shot him. But they were all there and were exceptionally heavy. They measured just over 54 inches on the curl—a very good bull.

I'd made my first safari to Africa the year before, and the two species I'd most wanted to collect were kudu and buffalo. When Cheri and I arrived in Maun, we were informed by the safari company that our hunt did not include kudu. We'd made arrangements before we'd

Russell Tarr and Cheri Flory with a good, heavy Zimbabwe kudu.

left the United States, and we had the paperwork to show that our safari *did* include kudu. "Tough luck" is what the company essentially said, however. But everyone else who had booked that same package safari *had* hunted kudu (we'd talked with six parties coming out). Apparently, the safari company had overbooked their quota on kudu, and I learned later that this wasn't an uncommon practice with this and some other safari companies. Unfortunately, it's something you have to worry about when booking an African safari, and it reflects on all of these companies, even very good ones like Umlali Safaris in Zimbabwe, who are very honest.

Since we'd already paid a 50 percent deposit and had spent a small fortune to get there, we really didn't have a choice. But our professional hunter, Willie Phillips, made up for all the hassle with the company. We had a phenomenal hunt and bagged nearly everything on our license. All were exceptional trophies as well, including that warthog I mentioned earlier. And to top it off, Willie arranged a kudu hunt for us independent of the safari company, and it was a successful one. We found a good bull, chased it down in savanna cover, and bagged it. It measured 52 inches on the curl. It was a pleasant way, indeed, to end up that hunt.

Most hunters going to southern Africa today plan on taking a kudu, and most succeed. The better places for the big, spiral-horned antelope include Zimbabwe (try Umlali Safaris; see the Appendix), Namibia (there are any number of good ranch hunts there), and the Republic of South Africa (likewise, if you don't mind contributing to apartheid), probably in that order. Zambia can be good, especially in the Luangwa Valley. David Petzal, executive editor of *Field & Stream*, bagged a kudu there that measured just a hair under 60 inches! That's a once-in-a-lifetime head, and Dave tells me he's since retired from kudu hunting.

Russell Tarr, our PH on the Zimbabwe safari, believes that the next world-record kudu will come from western Zimbabwe, and after seeing the bulls there, I wouldn't be the least bit surprised if he were right. One morning we saw four bulls within an hour and a half, one about 52 inches, another about 53, the third around 54, and another probably a fraction of an inch more than that. And that wasn't particularly unusual, either. If you hunted with Umlali Safaris on the Wight Farm, you could probably pick up a 50-inch bull within an hour. That's phenomenal kudu hunting! If I wanted another big kudu, that's exactly where I'd go.

13

The Sable Antelope

On my first Botswana safari, we several times saw herds of sable antelope while hunting plains game along the edge of the Okavango Delta. Unfortunately they weren't included on my license. In fact, I didn't know there were sable in the area until the hunt began. Even at that, it was hard not to think of shooting a big, black bull sable some day. Mature bulls are a glossy, obsidian black, with white undersides and white markings on the face. Younger bulls and cows are brown, ranging from a light, reddish brown to a dark chestnut that under certain light conditions look almost black. I decided on that hunt in Botswana that I would hunt sable first if I ever came back to Africa.

That morning Willie Phillips, our PH, found a herd of sable that contained a lone bull wildebeest. All we needed to finish off my license was to shoot that wildebeest. But I was so surprised by the magnificence of the bull sable as he stood in the early morning sun— Willie later estimated the length around the curve at 42 inches—that I forgot for a moment to look for the wildebeest. That moment was all he needed: The wildebeest bull, along with the entire herd of sable, whirled and trotted for the *Xuruxumb* trees. That was the last we ever saw of that wildebeest, and we never did find another bull.

Except for one immense, twisted-horned bull that lived alone near one of our camps, we never saw a bigger sable than that 42-incher. Sable in this region grazed in the open in the morning and evening and usually bedded in thin trees near their feeding areas during the day. It was easy to spot them in the shade of small stands or mopane or acacia as we hunted. Sable seemed to be creatures of habit, and if you saw one herd in a certain place on one day, the odds were very good they'd be in the same place the following day. A year later, the herds we watched in Zimbabwe behaved the same way. There was no sign of sable on the big islands out in the Okavango Delta, so apparently they are creatures of the dry savanna.

Most of my hunts in Africa took place in June. All of the adult bulls we saw in Zimbabwe had hind-leg injuries, so they must rut and battle sometime just before late June. Several people have told me about battling sable bulls, and apparently they're pretty fierce at times. They fight by going down on their front knees and hooking at each other's hindquarter, or anywhere else they can reach, with their vicious, big, black, scimitar-shaped horns.

The central African jungle-inhabiting bongo and the Ethiopian mountain nyala are the trophies to get if you've gone through Africa's list of more common game. But for those who haven't, the sable antelope probably ranks highest on the list. It was the reason I made a safari to Zimbabwe. Of the large antelope, the sable is valued most highly. For example, in 1990 the trophy fee for a kudu in Zimbabwe was five hundred dollars; for sable, fifteen hundred dollars; and for the large and spectacular gemsbok, where they are found, five hundred fifty dollars or less. The sable antelope is less widespread in southern Africa, where there is the best hunting and where most safaris are made these days; it's harder to come by than a kudu or gemsbok, so you pay for it. But if you get a good bull over 40 inches, he's worth the price.

Max Rosenfels, the owner of Umlali Safaris in Zimbabwe, told me when he was visiting the United States that I could expect to get a sable around 37 to 39 inches, since they didn't get particularly big in his area. Unlike most outfitters, African and North American alike, Max didn't exaggerate his hunting; in fact, as it turned out, he understated it by a mile. His soft-spoken manner and his references were largely the reasons I booked with him. Most outfitters are as soft-spoken as used-car salesmen, and they use the same hard-sell lines. Max, on the other hand, talked modestly about hunting other animals there, too.

Partly because Max understated the hunting, and partly because

I'd had bad luck with other outfitters, I didn't set my hopes too high. I'd have been happy with just a sable and perhaps one or two other antelope; I'd have been *ecstatic* with a sable and a leopard. As it turned out, I did a whole lot better than that—besides a sable and a leopard, I bagged a wildebeest, impala, reedbuck, bushbuck, waterbuck, and kudu, all record-class heads.

The sable hunt turned out to be a bit of an anticlimax. Back in the United States, I'd developed an obsession with obtaining one of those big, black antelope, and I seldom thought of anything else. As far as I was concerned, the hunt would be a failure if I didn't shoot a sable; everything else was unimportant.

It was the first animal we went after. Cheri and I drove out with Max to the Wight Farm; within an hour we had a 43-inch bull, about the largest ever taken from the place. We had driven up a dirt track on the farm. An old Matabele by the name of Petros spotted the chestnut brown of a cow sable in some acacia bush, and we noted others lying and browsing throughout the scrub. We drove past and found still more sable scattered through the savanna scrub. We found two small bulls, and then farther on, partially hidden in the thorn, was the tarry black of an adult bull. We couldn't get a good look at the bull's horns as he moved off slowly through the short trees and brush. There was a big bull in the area that had a broken horn, and Max thought this might be that one. But then the bull stepped out of the brush and turned a moment to look at us; both horns were intact and swept well back past the shoulder. I wasn't experienced with observing sable trophies, but the bull seemed at least as big as the one I'd seen in Botswana. Max, not one to get excited, watched the bull as he moved back behind more brush.

"I believe that is a good one," he said in his noncommittal way.

We stalked through the thornbush and high grass until the bull stood in the open again. "I think I'd take that one," Max said. I asked if the bull would go 40 inches and Max nodded.

I eased behind an acacia tree to close the distance and get a rest. The grass and scrub were at least belly-high, so I had to shoot standing to clear it. The bull moved off again, not fully frightened but a bit nervous. We followed, trying to get an open shot. Finally, after we had done more than a little jockeying for position, the bull walked out of the tree cover and across an opening. Sable are not as flighty or wary as many other antelope; a kudu bull, in comparison, would have taken off the moment we were out of the car.

The bull was quartering away slowly, occasionally looking back over his shoulder as we followed. The range was 175 yards. I steadied

I took this Zimbabwe sable (43 inches) in the first hour of the first safari day with outfitter and professional hunter Max Rosenfels. *Cheri Flory.*

myself and put the cross hairs just behind the rib cage so the slug would angle in forward to the lungs. The bull bucked at the blast of the .270 like a bronc just out of a rodeo chute, and he galloped into the trees. We circled to where the bull had gone. We found the rest of the herd, but he wasn't with them. We stalked back toward where I'd shot, and after about 150 yards, we found him stone dead. He was in poor condition and, like all the adult bulls we saw there, had an injured rear leg from rutting battles. The 150-grain bullet had entered just behind the rib cage and angled into the lungs, possibly nicking the heart. Big, bright, red-orange lung fragments hung on the high grass for 100 yards.

Back in camp, Max measured the bull at 43 inches, probably the largest taken there. I was ecstatic, and now I could relax since, as far as I was concerned, the safari was already a success.

Teddy Roosevelt, in his famous book *African Game Trails*, says that the sable is "the most beautiful animal next to the koodoo." I agree. He didn't hunt them on his safari to East Africa, but Kermit, his son, did. He killed a young bull and two cows, saying that one of the cows "when wounded was very savage, and tried to charge." In an antique shop in Bulawayo, Zimbabwe, I found a late nineteenth-century Boer diary in which the settler mentions a bull sable being attacked by his dogs. The bull killed two, one of which became firmly impaled on the bull's horns as he made his escape. The settler saw that sable some time later, and the dog, by then nearly mummified, was still on the bull's horns. In *The Green Hills of Africa*, Ernest Hemingway tells of being warned about keeping away from a sable's horns. Maj. Robert Foran, in his book *Kill: Or Be Killed*, was knocked over by a surprised bull he was attempting to photograph. He wasn't hurt, but from then on he was more cautious.

Sable are tough. *Field & Stream* editor Dave Petzal told me of a bull he'd killed in Zambia that had an old .375 bullet in its guts. The bull was in excellent condition nevertheless. Denis Lyell, who wrote *Memories of an African Hunter*, wounded a bull sable, but the animal jumped up and made its escape. He saw the bull some time later, and it appeared none the worse for having received a shot. Lyell estimated the bull at 50 inches. (Then, as now, it seems the biggest ones are those that get away!)

In his early twentieth-century book *Big Game Hunting In North-Eastern Rhodesia*, Owen Letcher says that sable were scarce in what is now Zambia, especially around the Luangwa Valley, which is famous safari country. As I understand it, today quite a few sable are taken out of Zambia, including the Luangwa Valley, so perhaps things have changed since Letcher's time. Zimbabwe, where I hunted sable, is another good area, and a few are also taken out of East Africa and Botswana. Safari operators tell me that the giant Angola sable is now illegal to hunt.

On my Zimbabwe safari, Max Rosenfels told me I could shoot another sable if I wanted, since I'd taken the first so quickly and easily. Wildlife in Zimbawe is considered the property of the landowners, who can pretty much do what they want with it. Because wild game is a constant source of income for Zimbabwe, it's allowed to stay on private lands even if it competes with cattle. If not for the hunters bringing money to the country and the landowners, there'd be little left of Zimbabwe's wildlife today; the game would be an economic liability since it competes for grazing areas with cattle. I was happy

My collection of Zimbabwe trophies. *Cheri Flory.*

enough with the sable I had taken, and I didn't really have a strong
desire to shoot another. (I have to admit that I was also thinking about
that extra fifteen-hundred-dollar trophy fee.)

Later, while hunting with Russell Tarr, we found another very big
sable. Russell thought the horns were as long as those of my bull,
though I didn't agree, but it definitely was a heavier animal. Its right
rear leg was fractured, and I considered shooting it just to put it out of
its misery. But Russell thought the bull might survive, as there were
no hyenas or lions there, having been long ago exterminated by
farmers, and leopards had better sense than to attack an adult sable,
even a wounded one. I decided to let it go, and even today I have
mixed feelings about it. I may never get another chance at sable that
big. If I think about it, I can still see the cross hairs solidly on that
bull's shoulder as I rested the rifle across an acacia branch and tried to
make up my mind. And I recall the heavy sweep of the polished black

horns, the afternoon sun glistening on the black sheen of his coat, and myself, with mixed feelings, thumbing the safety back on and turning away.

Of all the species of African game I've collected on the savanna, the one I'd most like to hunt again is the sable antelope.

14

The Aptly Named Bushbuck

The bushbuck is a shy, secretive animal that hides to avoid detection. Only after it thinks it's been spotted or when it's certain it can escape will it run. It is a small, reddish antelope dappled with white spots. It has striped markings on the face, black legs, and thick, spiraled, ivory-tipped black horns. Its name is highly appropriate, because it hides in large bushes and relies on its camouflage dappling to make it invisible among the leaves. From my reading and my experience, it seems that all varieties of bushbuck inhabit thick, dense forest and brush near water or dry watercourses. In southern Zimbabwe, this thick fringe of trees and vegetation along rivers, even rivers that have been dry for years, is called *riverine*.

Hunting bushbuck is in some ways similar to stalking mule deer, whitetails, or elk in timber. You have to sneak and/or track slowly along, keeping aware of what's ahead, watching the wind, and moving as slowly and quietly as you can. One difference with the bushbuck, however, is that it's better hidden when it's standing in the heavy canopy of a large bush or shrub. And another important difference to North American hunters is that while sneaking through timber after a big buck or bull in Wisconsin or Wyoming, you don't have to worry about running into spitting Mozambique cobras, puff adders, scorpions, or venomous spiders.

The bushbuck pays little attention to what it hears unless it can correlate the sound with smell or sight. Several times three or four of us have stalked up on bedded bulls (sometimes also called rams) that easily could hear us forcing our way through the thick tangle. They didn't break and run for it until they spotted us. Frequently males saw us and froze just where they were, confident of their ability to remain undetected. Once we approached within twenty yards of a male as he hid in a thick bush. Only his legs and lower chest were visible in the branches just below the crown of foliage, so we couldn't judge his horns. Finally he broke and ran for it, and though I didn't have time for a shot, we all saw that his horns were very good. In a moment he was swallowed up by the vines and thorns and became one of several that got away on that hunt.

While stalking buffalo, lechwe, and other game in the Okavango, we several times found bushbuck hiding in the brush or forest along the channels of the swamp. Willie Phillips, my PH on the Okavango safari, said that few people, including the game department, realized the numbers of bushbuck in parts of the delta. Some of the islands in the Okavango hold enormous populations of bushbuck that never get hunted.

In Zimbabwe, we spent several days hunting bushbuck on the way back from stalking some other beast. The first time we tried it, we stalked through the riverine tangle of tall grass and weeds, vines, immense acacia trees, thorny and thick acacia brush, and other various thorns and nettles. Spiders and small creatures dropped from the bush onto my head and down my neck. Once a scorpion dropped onto my shoulder, and I was so anxious to get rid of it that I jumped into a "wait-a-bit" thorn. Russell Tarr hated that kind of stalking and had a phobia about spiders. Spiders didn't bother me, but I didn't really care for the ticks. These were abundant, from larvae so small they were invisible, to slightly larger larvae that were barely detectable with the human eye, and then only if they moved, to big, dark, shiny adults that looked just like the kind in the Rockies. My fear was well-founded, too. Both Cheri and I came down with South African tick fever, a disease that, if left untreated, can be fatal. Fortunately I'd read about Lyme disease in *Outdoor Life* before I'd left the States and suspected that the chills, fever, dizziness, and aches—the early stages of the disease—were caused by tick bites. A couple weeks of doxycycline kicked it, however, and within a month or so we were nearly as fit as ever.

Several times on the stalk we jumped bushbuck, but there was never time enough to make a decently placed shot or, for that matter, adequately judge the trophy. Once, while we were off stalking through the thick bush, two trophy males walked within thirty yards of the Land Cruiser where Cheri and one of the staff waited. The bushbuck paused in the track long enough for any number of shots. We didn't see any other bushbuck that day, either.

While stalking the dainty, quick antelope, Russell several times warned me about walking up on a wounded bushbuck. Russell had read of several people who'd been killed or severely wounded by them within recent years. Having seen how tiny they were—less than a hundred pounds on the hoof for a big male—and having hunted grizzlies, Cape buffalo, and a leopard, it was a bit hard for me to take this antelope too seriously.

When I got back to the United States, I read up on bushbucks. Denis Lyell wrote in *Memories of an African Hunter* that he had "read in a South African newspaper . . . of a white man being killed by a ram . . . which attacked him and punctured him in the stomach." Lyell also had his own close call with a bushbuck. He'd grabbed by the horns one that he'd shot and taken for dead. The bushbuck almost threw Lyell off his feet. He continues: "I knew if I let go of the horns, I should probably get them in the stomach, so I hung on." The ram was badly wounded through both lungs, and Lyell notes that "had he happened to be only slightly wounded, I am sure I could not have held him."

The bushbuck was and is a prized trophy. Owen Letcher (*Big Game Hunting in North-Eastern Rhodesia*) shot a ram along the Luangwa River in what is now Zambia. The ram measured 11½ inches around the spiral of the horn, apparently quite a good ram for that country, according to Letcher, who remarks that "a good head is always deemed a prize." Letcher also writes, "When wounded, a bushbuck ram is a most dangerous little beast . . . and their charge is incredibly swift."

Edouard Foá, a French explorer-hunter, killed a bushbuck in central Africa that measured 12 inches. He doesn't seem greatly impressed with hunting bushbuck, though, because he has almost nothing to say about them.

Our last day at the Bubi River safari camp in Zimbabwe, I almost didn't try hunting them. We'd already taken a good leopard and an immense waterbuck there, and I'd been considering returning to our first camp in the dry kopje country up north to try for another leopard—the big one that had given us the slip on our second night in the blind. (Now, a year later, Russell Tarr tells me that that leopard has since killed twenty-eight calves.) Bushbuck wasn't really high on my list of priorities. But almost as an afterthought, I decided to devote one full day to hunting the little antelope. And I'm glad I did! Driving along the river, which had been dry for four or five years, we saw a herd of nyalas, then protected. Several times herds of impalas leapt across the track and into the forest, and we saw several female bushbuck. Twice we spotted good males in the bush, but before we could stop the Land Cruiser and get out to shoot, they were off.

Shorty, an old, crafty, and cocky Matabele, was the head tracker at the Bubi River Camp. He rapped on the roof of the cab with his knuckles, and before it came to a stop, he was out examining some tracks in the dust, at the same time motioning to me. He took off at a trot and I followed, before Russell, Cheri, or the other trackers could even climb out. I was glad we were alone, because I'd already seen Shorty at work spooring, and he was more than just a mere master of the art; it was almost as though he were practicing voodoo as he unraveled the trail and anticipated what the beast was doing. For the first time there were only the two of us, not half a dozen, and we were hunting together. I really doubted that it was possible to stalk bushbuck in that riverine tangle with more people, as our past experience had proved, and I felt confident for the first time.

Shorty followed the tracks quickly, at the same time scanning ahead. It takes practice even to see a hiding bushbuck when someone is pointing it out, and it takes years of stalking them to be able to find them before they run. Lone bushbuck lie underneath heavy bushes, and if there's danger, they stand up. When they're standing, most of their body is hidden in the leaves of the bushes and their legs look like branches. I'd started being able to find them on my own, but I would never find them before Shorty did.

Shorty slowed slightly, stopped and pointed, then motioned me to rest the rifle over his shoulder. The ram took off, and we trotted after it. Perhaps uncharacteristically, the ram stopped in the cover of bush and turned to look. He was standing quartering away at a sharp angle in the less dense vegetation on a high bank of the sand river. I put the .270 across Shorty's shoulder, got a sight picture through the branches, and touched off. The bushbuck stumbled at the shot, regained his feet, and bounded off through the brushy tangle. Shorty ran to head him off, and I followed. We had run for 150 yards when we both saw the bushbuck standing in more brush, this time not completely hiding himself. He had to be hard hit to stand in the open like that. I held on his shoulder offhand, hoping the bullet wouldn't be deflected by a branch, and slapped the trigger. The animal collapsed, and both Shorty and I ran up to it.

As we approached and could see the ram, Shorty grabbed my hand and squeezed it. The old cynic was excited—the one and only time I'd seen him that way on the hunt (he didn't even get too worked up over the leopard)—and he kept telling me how big it was. In my vast bushbuck stalking experience, it looked the same as the others we'd seen. But it wasn't. The beautiful, black, ivory-tipped, spiral horns measured a hair's breadth short of 17 inches, and they were heavy.

Top Matabele tracker Shorty with 17-inch Limpopo bushbuck, the largest ever taken from that safari camp.

A very fat Botswana zebra.

Russell, always an excitable fellow when game is taken, was beside himself as he whooped and hollered and did a little dance. Later, after the initial adrenaline rush had worn down, Russell mentioned he thought it would be the biggest taken in Zimbabwe that year. He and Pierre later green-scored it. They believed it would go somewhere between numbers 8 and 12 in the SCI record book. That didn't really make a bit of difference to me; actually, I would have been just as happy with a smaller bushbuck, as long as it was mature. But records seem to be the standard by which trophies are judged, and everyone's excitement over the ram contributed to my own appreciation of it and to my sense of triumph. It was really Shorty who had gotten that ram, however; all I had done was press the trigger.

When I had left for that Zimbabwe safari, I couldn't have cared less whether or not I got a bushbuck. Now, after having hunted them, I look forward to getting the mount back from the taxidermist almost as much as I do the leopard and the sable, and I have fond memories of how much fun it was to hunt them.

Part III
Mountain Game

Mountain game species include all varieties of mountain sheep and mountain goats. Mountain sheep are the most sought after and valuable trophy in North America, and the hunter who has a big ram or two in his trophy room has achieved a higher status because of them. A big billy goat isn't considered as spectacular a trophy as a good ram is, even though goats live in tougher country and are less widespread than sheep. A good goat with 10-inch horns will get little more than a yawn from the uninitiated visitor to your trophy room. Hunting goats, too, is apt to be dangerous. Mountain goats are best characterized perched on a slender ledge on the face of a vertical, two-thousand-foot cliff; they are the true climbers of mountain game. Sheep bound and hop from foothold to foothold, whereas goats are slow, deliberate, technical scalers and go places that would kill a sheep.

But mountain game is not just sheep and goats. Grizzlies, mule deer, elk, and caribou aren't generally thought of as being high-mountain game, but in certain places and at certain times, they inhabit country as high as or higher than do mountain sheep. For example, one season in the Brooks Range was hot and dry. Botflies and warble flies in the valleys were driving caribou mad, so as a consequence hundreds of bulls lined the steep, blade-edged, rocky ridges of the highest peaks while sheep grazed in basins below them. And I've hunted mule deer in September in the Montana and Wyoming Rockies at eleven thousand feet, well above timberline, while goats wandered the peaks around them and sheep grazed in cliffside meadows below. At these times you hunt deer or elk just as you would a wise, old bighorn sheep, stalking them with great respect for their vision, always staying out of sight.

Approaching mule deer can be nerve-racking: Their sense of smell is among the best, they have perhaps the best hearing of any North American game animal, and their vision seems as good as that of pronghorns or sheep. When stalking them you must take all senses into account: Stay out of sight, keep quiet, and approach upwind. High-country caribou are less cagey and wary than mule deer, mainly because they're not hunted as hard, so they're easier to kill.

Throughout the Rockies, grizzlies spend much of their waking season in high country grazing on lush, alpine meadow herbage, digging for ground squirrels and marmots, and scavenging for goat or sheep carcasses at the base of avalanche channels and cliffs. And in some parts of the Far North, grizzlies stay high in mountain valleys well above timberline until a month or so before denning time. So the best way to hunt bears at these times and places is to go high.

The grizzly's eyesight isn't as good as that of other mountain game, so when hunting them there's less need to stay out of sight. Bears' vision is much better than they are generally given credit for, however. I once had a high-country grizzly pick me out at five hundred yards on an open tundra basin, and another time one spotted me three hundred yards away in waist-high Arctic dwarf birch. They can also pick out movement surprisingly well.

Besides the fact that the mountains offer good hunting, with some species found nowhere else, there is a more important consideration for hunting in the high country: Mountains are the closest our planet reaches to heaven.

15

Mountain Sheep

There are probably more fanatical sheep hunters than for any other species, with the possible exception of whitetails. Part of this lies in how impressive an adult ram is as a trophy: There's something truly sensuous in a heavy, battered, wrinkled, and weathered set of horns from an old ram. There are few days when I don't put my hand on the horns of a big Stone sheep that hangs near the door to my study, feel the heavy creases of its annual rings, trace my finger into and out of a big chunk that was broken out in some battle, run my hand along the length of its curl.

Sheep inhabit the wildest and most remote lands left on the planet—places of clear and clean air, pure streams, and untouched forests. There's something special about climbing a peak in the Far North where no man has ever set foot and staring off through air that is so clear you can see a hundred miles away.

Sheep live from near sea-level altitudes along the Sea of Cortez in Sonora, Mexico, to twelve thousand feet in the Rocky Mountains. Desert bighorn sheep can tolerate temperatures in excess of 125°F in the Sonora Desert and southwestern mountain ranges, and northern varieties of sheep live comfortably in temperatures way below zero. I once watched some Dall sheep grazing contentedly on a mountain slope in the Brooks Range in late December, while the thermometer outside my tent read $-69°F$!

Basically, North American sheep can live in all kinds of habitats as long as there is rough escape terrain near at hand. The key to whether sheep inhabit a particular mountain range is the presence of escape terrain. Sheep aren't fast runners—even a lame, old wolf can run one down without much trouble—so they must rely on rough, steep, rocky country for safety. Wolves, bears, or mountain lions won't bother a ram if he's on a steep, rocky slope. The feet of predator species have soft pads that are susceptible to injury on sharp rocks, while sheep have hard, horny hooves ideal for climbing. In addition, a sheep can trot up a steep, seventy-five-degree slope without so much as breathing hard, yet if a wolf or grizzly tries this, it will be panting for all it's worth within a few minutes.

I observed a subadult grizzly chase some rams that were grazing in an open tundra basin. The rams watched as the bear approached, and once they were satisfied it was up to no good, they trotted to the nearest rocky slide chute and climbed a few yards up it. The bear was young and foolish, and he continued after the rams. They weren't much worried, and they climbed another thirty yards up the rocks and turned to look at the bear fifty yards below. The bear kept coming until it was only twenty yards away—it must have been famished for red meat. The rams filed a few yards higher through the scree jumble, then again turned to stare at the bear. The bear kept at it, though by then it was laboring heavily. The rams seemed highly amused, and they never did show any real concern. They led that foolish bear all the way up that rock slide, and the bear's tongue was hanging nearly to the ground as it panted its way over the ridge.

Most predators aren't foolish enough to waste energy chasing sheep once they hit the rocks, however. I once saw two wolves approach a group of old, trophy rams in an Arctic basin. The sheep dashed for a steep, rocky slope, trotted thirty yards up it to a long ledge, and turned to watch. As soon as the rams reached the rocks, the wolves pulled up and trotted off in another direction as if to say they hadn't really wanted mutton, anyway.

Although most predators won't look twice at sheep on steep slopes, sheep are easy prey in flat country. As an illustration of how slow sheep are on the flats, I once witnessed a wolf run down a band of lambs and ewes that were migrating from the north slope of the Alaska Range along Sanctuary River to the south slope of the Outer Range in Alaska's Denali National Park. The medium-sized wolf had no trouble running down and killing an old ewe at the tail end of the band. It finished with the first ewe, then left it and went after the band, which was by then galloping along the rocky, braided channel of the glacial river. The wolf caught another ewe without much trouble and dispatched it, too. It let the rest of the sheep go, but I'm sure it could have killed them all before they made it to the rocky safety of the Outer Range two miles away. I suspect that the wolf was one of a pack that had a den farther up the river and that the mutton was destined for the pups.

Sheep are migratory animals and, like mule deer, change home ranges with the season. Sheep are generally loyal to a home range and return to it in the same season year after year. On my first hunt for Stone sheep in the Toad River drainage on the east slope of the Rockies, Ralph Kitchen, my guide, was familiar with almost every ram of the forty or so we saw on the hunt. Year after year, certain rams would be in a place he called the Fish Bowl. You hunted them there by sneaking across the top of a plateau to the rim of a steep canyon, spotting the rams, then sneaking down on them. Ralph said it was like shooting fish in a bowl, hence, the name. Among these rams was a very old one Ralph called Stubby. Ralph said he was at least fourteen years old at the time. He had short, stubby horns—no trophy, so no hunter would shoot him. He was the largest ram through the body we saw on that hunt, and he did no breeding. Ralph had taken hunters into the place several times and shot rams out of Stubby's band. But Stubby kept coming back.

Valerius Geist writes in his book *Mountain Sheep* that in late September and early October, bighorn sheep move to their winter, prerut home ranges; in late October and early November, rams move to the rutting grounds; in late December, they migrate from rutting grounds to their wintering home ranges; and in late May through early July, they travel to summer ranges. Some rams may summer with the same rams on a given meadow each year but then travel to a completely different autumn home range, which may be in mountains twenty miles away from where the rest of the band goes.

I've found, however, that mature rams of nine or older aren't particularly faithful to their late summer home range in much of Alaska. The hunting season opens in early August, and rams are on their summer range then. I seldom see the same rams in a given area year after year, though that place is obviously a ram summer area. Last season we spotted twenty-nine rams in a small mountain range. Twenty of these rams were legal, seven-eighths-curl animals, and at

Two good Alaska Range Dall rams.

least six of them were real, old trophies. We saw only one ewe with a lamb that summer.

But those Dall rams are, I'm reasonably sure, an exception to the rule; rams in other places do seem to be faithful to seasonal home ranges. Perhaps those Dall rams aren't faithful to limited, seasonal home ranges because the place has short summers and short growing seasons, and they must wander widely to find enough high-quality grazing. I can remember only two rams returning to the same valley on two consecutive summers. One was an old ram with very distinctive, wide, flaring horns. I'd seen him the preceding summer in a band of four adults.

Early in my sheep-hunting career, I spotted an immense ram of at least 43 inches, with one broken horn. I hunted that ram religiously for years afterward as if he were the Golden Fleece and the Holy Grail rolled into one. I never did see that ram again, though, and I passed up some very big sheep while searching for him. He was one of those rams that didn't return to the same home range, though it's possible he had died over the winter.

Normally the largest-horned male is the dominant ram in a band. Rams with smaller horns bow to his status symbols and follow him. The exception is when a big-horned ram is sick or injured; then, subordinates beat on him unmercifully. Overt aggression is nearly always initiated by a subordinate ram—one lower in the hierarchy—so if a dominant ram is injured or ill, younger rams quickly find out about it.

The dominant ram in a group treats all lesser sheep just as he would females and frequently mounts subordinates to keep them in their place. Rams may battle at any time of year, not just during the rut, and they do so more to determine their place in the pecking order than to compete for a comely ewe. Rams that are familiar with one another know just where they stand, so serious battles seldom occur. When there *is* a serious fight, it's usually between two rams of equal or near-equal status that haven't yet decided which is boss or between two strange rams that have not battled before.

Lone rams frequently are those that are injured or too old to put up with the constant testing and sparring in a ram group. Of the two lone rams I've killed, one had been injured in a fall—the tip of one horn was freshly broken, facial hair had been scraped off, and he was badly bruised along the ribs—and the other was simply old and lame and unable to hold his own in a ram group. Rams at least partially determine their status in a group by displaying horns to each other. I have watched pairs of bighorn or Dall rams stand for hours with their horns together, occasionally turning their heads a bit so a competitor could get a better view.

Sheep are active at night. I've watched them graze and cavort all night long in the very far north where it didn't get fully dark in early or middle August. At first I thought it was because, with the per-petual daylight, they could see to graze, display, and spar. But I've also listened to Dall sheep fight in the darkness, the loud, rifle-shot *pop* of their horns echoing through the subzero Yukon night in the mountains along Kluane Lake. I've seen them along the Alaskan Highway on dark nights, as well, and I've seen bighorn rams cross the road at night while tending ewes along Yellowstone National Park's Gardiner River.

The implication for hunters is that, more often than not, rams are going to be bedded during daylight hours, though they may get up and graze for short periods. In order to locate rams, you'll need to glass likely looking bedding areas, which include rocky outcrops where visibility is good and the wind is strong, particularly if it's warm and insects are thick; shady north slopes if temperatures are high; caves or fractures in cliffs if it's hot, very windy, or stormy; and rocky outcrops in timber if rams are heavily hunted, as they are in Montana's "open sheep areas."

Sheep that have been heavily hunted have learned to seek the timber like members of the deer family do. Bighorns hide in stands of conifers in overhunted parts of Montana, British Columbia, and almost all sheep areas in Alberta. I've also watched Dall sheep in country where they've never been shot at run into caves because of a low-flying bush plane. Mostly, though, sheep are open-country animals.

Individual rams that grow the most rapidly in both body and horn size breed earlier and hence die younger, because they enter the winter with their fat reserves depleted from the rigors of rutting. Conversely, rams with poorer early growth live longer, since their horns aren't big enough to enable them to become primary breeders until much later in life. According to Geist, the oldest rams in a population are characterized by small body and horn size. The part about horn size holds true for that Toad River ram Stubby, but not the part about body size. Another exception was the last ram I killed, a thirteen-year-old—a very ancient ram, particularly for the far north climate and the wolf-infested country. He was not a small ram, even though he was very old. He was obviously larger in the body than the other rams in his group, one of which was a full-curl ram about nine years old. He was a bit lame, though he was still the dominant male of the band, and it was likely he wouldn't make it through the long, harsh Arctic winter. I was happy to get him for more than one reason.

Factors involved in horn growth include heredity, the ewe's health while she was pregnant, the male lamb's health and nutrition, the condition of grazing plants in any given year (drought adversely affects plant growth, of course, and consequently an animal's health), injuries, and illnesses. I have several sheep trophies on which the annual growth rings for two or more seasons are quite close together. This means that the ram had probably been injured or ill during this time, and all of his energy was going toward repairing the body, not horn growth. Sheep horns grow throughout the summer when grazing is good and stop growing during the winter when rams are on survival rations, at which time deep annual growth rings are formed.

The four varieties of North American sheep are lumped into two groups: the bighorns and the thinhorns. The thinhorns include the Dall and Stone sheep, and the bighorns include both varieties of bighorn sheep. The horns of bighorns are often much heavier than those of either Dall or Stone rams, though they're usually not as long. Over the years I've seen several bighorn heads with 17-inch-plus bases that were bagged in restricted hunt areas in the Butte, Montana, vicinity. The heaviest Dall I've ever taken had a 14¼-inch base. The heaviest Stone ram I've bagged also had a 14¼-inch base. This is fairly heavy for thinhorns.

Except for desert bighorns, North American sheep rut in late November and into December. The odds are against longevity in rams. While chasing ewes up and down mountainsides and fending off competitors, they lose much of the fat reserves built up during the summer. Then they enter the harsh, unforgiving northland or mountain winter in a run-down condition. Most rams, particularly those that have the largest horns and do most of the rutting, die during the winter when grazing is hard to find. Being a trophy ram is not an easy way to live; if the rutting, winter, or wolves don't kill you, a hunter will. But at least in that case your horns will become a symbol, a shrine, a memorial.

Where to go for a trophy ram? If you're after Dalls, the place to hunt for a real trophy is Canada's Northwest Territories, specifically the Mackenzie Mountains. Ralph Kitchen guided for an outfitter there, and his clients took several 40-inch plus rams. I've met other hunters who have taken very good sheep from the same area. Probably the Yukon is the second best place for a good Dall. In both areas, success rates on good sheep are high, often around 100 percent in the Northwest Territories. Alaska these days is overhunted, and outfitters aren't very selective; anything legal will do. I talked with two Brooks Range outfitters last year and both were running 60 to 70 percent success. One had taken rams of from 31 to 36 inches, and another of 32 to 36. Those aren't big sheep, even though they did make the 7/8 curl legal limit. The story is the same in the Alaskan Range, though the rams average larger.

Stone sheep hunting is best on the east slope of the Rockies, and places like the Toad River drainage and surrounding country are good. Rams tend to be darker on the east slope, as opposed to some that are so light that a shoulder mount is almost indistinguishable from a Dall sheep shoulder mount. Both types are found on the east slope, however. Outfitters out of Ft. Nelson, Pink Mountain, and nearby northeast British Columbia towns are good bets, but check references carefully. First obtain a list of Stone sheep outfitters from the British Columbia Ministry of Environment.

The biggest bighorn sheep anywhere are coming out of Montana.

Top Canadian Stone and Dall sheep guide Ralph Kitchen with huge Northwest Territories Dall ram. *Ralph Kitchen.*

Drawing areas around Anaconda, Missoula, and Butte regularly produce huge rams in the 195 Boone-and-Crockett point category, some with bases as big around as your thigh: They dwarf even the largest Stone or Dall sheep. It's tough to get a permit though. There's always some difficulty, but all you can do is put in for one in the annual drawings. Bighorn hunting in Alberta, a once famous bighorn country, and British Columbia has deteriorated over the years. The chief problem there is competition with resident hunters, who are always spoiling a stalk or chasing sheep off. It seems in many if not most hunting areas, residents don't have to draw for a limited number of permits. They just walk in and buy one. Consequently there's too much hunting pressure in the hills and few real trophies. Wyoming is a good bet for a decent ram, and the areas to the east and southeast of Yellowstone Park have good odds for drawing a permit. Usually your odds are one out of twenty or one out of thirty. Outfitters in these areas are running very high hunter success, too. The rams, however, don't achieve the size of their Montana cousins.

Your best and probably cheapest chance for a desert sheep is in Baja, Mexico. The last time I checked, hunts were running around thirteen thousand dollars, and success fairly was good, though nowhere near 100 percent. A few years ago, demand was low enough that you could simply buy a hunt. Now, you must draw for a limited number of tags, though your chances for success are much higher than any drawings in the United States. A warning: I have heard some horror stories about Mexican hunts from very disgruntled hunters.

Most drawing areas in Arizona have odds as high as a hundred to one against drawing. Of course some are slightly better. Arizona's drawing system has recently become more complicated too, with points given for all sorts of things to increase the chances of getting a permit. If you buy a hunting license, you're given points. It's to the point that Arizona (as well as other states) are making hunter drawings into big business (after all, they keep your fees for months, making enormous interest off of them before they return them to the mostly unsuccessful hunters; now, if you buy certain things, you get bonus points, and the state makes more money).

Nevada has fewer desert sheep but the application procedure and drawings are simpler. If you really want a sheep, you can buy a hunt on the Hualapai Indian Reservation in the Grand Canyon for about twenty thousand dollars, too. But spending that much money on a hunt for one animal gives me sweaty palms. I'd probably blow the shot, I'd be so nervous.

16

The Hardy Dall Sheep

I saw my first live Dall sheep in the Outer Range of Denali National Park in Alaska in 1980. I'd first located them from the valley floor, and since one of the things I wanted most from that trip was a photo of a good Dall ram, I planned a sneak to get within photo range. I was successful and did manage to get some good shots. After a while, the band of rams accepted me and I was able to edge into their midst. There were sheep on all sides of me, several within four or five yards. I even managed to set up the camera, activate the timer, and get a photo of me sitting among the rams.

From that time on I've had a love affair with Dall sheep. I stalk and photograph them each summer in the Alaska and Brooks ranges of Alaska, and I hunt them occasionally. I even bought some land and built a couple of cabins to be near sheep.

Dalls inhabit the harshest environment on earth. They live out their lives among the highest peaks and mountain ranges of the very far north. In the Brooks Range, the actual summer and growing season may be less than two months and there may be snow on the ground for ten. Sheep have to do their growing and replenish fat reserves lost during the long winter in those two months or so.

The hunting season in the Arctic begins in early August. At that time, there's no darkness that far north, and sheep frequently graze much of the night. Then, night is the best time to hunt, since it's cooler, there are fewer flies and mosquitoes, and Dall sheep are more active. The summer there is a pleasant time. It's usually not too hot, though there have been rare seasons when I've hunted sheep in safari shorts, and the nights are cool and comfortable. On the other hand, you may wind up hunting in a foot of snow. Normally the tundra is beginning to die and turn tawny and wine colored.

The sheep season ends in mid-September, though during the last part of the hunt there's usually too much snow and the weather is too bad for hunting in the mountains. Sheep stay high, although they migrate to a different home range once the snows come. And they stay high all winter, living comfortably (if that's possible!) above valley ice fogs and wolves and surviving temperatures of − 80°F. If you're traveling in the far north wilderness during winter, carrying a small thermometer can be a lifesaving thing to do; you don't want to be outdoors when the mercury drops below − 50°F. The Dall sheep is the most numerous and widespread of North America's wild sheep, though even on the southern edge of its range−the southern Yukon Territory, the Kenai Peninsula in south Alaska, and the Chugach Mountains−the climate and terrain are still harsh. They must be tough creatures!

Dall or other mountain sheep seldom rely on hearing to detect danger. Their ears are small in comparison with those of animals that rely heavily on hearing, such as mule deer or kudu. The muley's ears are easily four times the size of the ram's ears, even though both animals are about the same in body size. Usually by the time the sheep can hear a wolf or a man, it's too late. Instead, they rely on eyesight to detect predators long before they can hear them. As a result, sheep bed on promontories or other places where they have a good view of the most likely approaches. Hunting mountain sheep involves staying out of sight, using the topography to your advantage to get within rifle range, and making a clean shot.

Rams are located mostly by glassing with binoculars; then the trophy is judged and the approach route is planned with a spotting scope. Where I used to hunt Dall sheep, I had to fly two hours in a tiny, cramped Cessna 185; float downriver for several days in an inflatable raft on a wild, glacial river; backpack for several more up a long canyon; and trek on foot twenty-five miles a day as I hunt. A spotting scope, therefore, was a luxury I couldn't afford to carry. I had to rely instead on compact binoculars, with which judging trophies at two

I don't always hunt. Here I take behavioral notes on a ram band in the Brooks Range in midsummer.

miles is tough. So, I've learned to rely on subtle hints as to the size of a ram. A big ram is chunkier and blockier than a small ram and walks in a more assured and fluid manner, since he's probably the dominant ram of the band and is sure of his place in the pecking order. If you can see a ram's horns at all at two miles, or even some distance less, he's apt to be an adult, and any fully adult ram (nine years or older in the Far North) is worth investigating. True, I do have to make more approaches and sneaks before I finally settle on a trophy, but that's the price a hunter must pay when hunting in places others don't go.

In parts of their range, Dalls are the easiest of the mountain sheep to locate. In Denali National Park, for example, Dalls are obvious white specks against the verdant tundra slopes, dark shale, or brown volcanic rock. In parts of the Brooks Range, however, they can be harder to see than the bighorns in Montana. There are many white or whitish rocks in parts of the Brooks, and sheep are often soiled so badly they appear brown or dirty white at a distance, so they too often blend into their surroundings.

Glassing takes patience and faith. When I stalk a place where I've seen rams in earlier years, I take my time and glass every nook and cranny thoroughly, wait, then glass the area again. Because I've seen rams there before, I have the faith to continue glassing when I could be still-hunting up the next canyon. I've too often glassed right over entire bands of rams that were bedded in the open, only to spot them an hour later when one ram gets up to change position or nibble a bit of tundra. Sometimes a change of angle in the sun illuminates a horn or flank you hadn't seen before, and it frequently causes a change in shadow pattern, making a ram that was completely invisible a mile earlier seem so obvious you wonder how you could have missed him the first time around.

Once you've found likely looking rams, it's important to plan the sneak and approach carefully. Go over the terrain foot by foot with binoculars or spotting scope. That ravine across the canyon that leads up to that ram may look deep enough to conceal you, but it may not be once you get there. Look more carefully, especially at shadows along or in it. Try to gauge its depth and concealment potential by willow bushes, spruce trees, or other animals.

There are often no trees or brush for concealment, so a hunter has to rely on hills, ridges, gullies, and anything else uneven in that sheep country's mostly uneven topography. Vegetation is seldom more than shin-high, and even on the valley floors the highest brush is waist-high dwarf Arctic birch and willow scrub. Too frequently there is no cover in which to stalk up on a group of rams, and a hunter has to either approach in the open from below or leave them and try again some other time.

I once stalked some rams that were high on a short ledge across a canyon. The stalk seemed easy. All I'd have to do was cross the valley floor, work my way up a steep avalanche chute, then ease across an open tundra slope that should be out of the rams' line of vision. If it worked out, I'd get within fifty or sixty yards. Everything went according to plan except the last part. I'd eased to within sixty yards or so, all right, but the rams were on the ledge just above and were thus invisible. They might as well have been on the next planet. By the time I'd climbed back down to the valley floor, the rams had gotten up and were grazing over the crest of the ridge, and there wasn't time enough that day for another stalk. That was the last I saw of those sheep, too.

Though sheep don't rely heavily on scent to detect danger, on occasion it does tip off a ram. But the quirky mountain zephyrs are generally too shifty and unreliable to be of much use to sheep. If you're stalking rams from below, keep in mind that when the air warms during the day it becomes less dense, rises, and blows up the mountain. You may need to plan your stalk from another direction. Last season I didn't and lost a 40-incher because of it.

We'd seen the rams the day before, and I'd botched a stalk on them. We found them again that morning several miles away, on the shoulder of a steep, rocky peak I called Dark Mountain. We sat on the spongy tundra in the sun, watching the rams from more than a mile away as we ate our lunches. I wanted to wait them out. They eventually had to come out of the rocks and off the cliffs to feed in the tundra at the base of the mountain, or so I reasoned. But there was no telling how long they'd stay high, so we went after them. We gave it a try against my better judgment, since it's no fun lying in the mountain wind, even in the sun, for ten to twelve hours waiting on sheep.

It took us about three hours to climb up to the sheep. We first crossed the valley floor, then got out of sight behind some ridges. We hiked along the base of the peak to a steep avalance chute that led up into the cliffs. We stalked up the chute, out of the rams' line of vision, climbing through van-sized boulders many of which were just at the angle of repose (which means they were about ready to roll into the valley below). Some teetered with our weight. The ravine steepened until we had to climb with hands and feet. There were freshly churned rocks and rock slivers from the frequent avalanches that rumbled down the chute, and we kept a wary eye on the cliffs above. I was extremely nervous about the place. We continued up the 80-degree chute where it went through a thick layer of rock until we were on top of cliffs. We then angled along the top toward the rams, which were, I calculated, a few hundred yards abreast of us. The rams heard us when we were within sixty or seventy yards, but they didn't run. If I raised my head, I could just see the smallest of the rams at the head of a small but steep gully. Apparently the other rams were just below. I eased toward them on the shaky, noisy rock, when an errant zephyr fanned the back of my sweaty neck. The sheep suddenly appeared, milled about for a moment, so tightly gathered that I couldn't tell which was the big one, then ran in a bunch around the curve of the slope. That was the last of them, too, and I cursed fluently as I sat on a boulder and stared out over those wild valleys thousands of feet below. I've seldom felt more dejected.

I bagged my largest ram during a more typical sheep hunt. I'm

Dall ram in the Alaska Range.

quick to come up with a name for a new piece of country, and I later named the barren, jagged canyon up which I was hiking Trophy Creek, for reasons that will become obvious. It had been a long, tough hunt. I'd spent some of that time in a tiny backpacking tent, but most of it had been spent trekking twenty or more miles a day up and down tundra and rock, searching for rams. Early in the hunt I'd passed up several full-curl rams searching for that monster 43-plus-incher I mentioned earlier, and it had been several days since I'd even seen a legal ram. I was nearly out of food and I needed meat badly, so I made up my mind to take any legal ram I could. I decided to hike back to a small canyon where I'd seen a legal ram earlier in the hunt. He wasn't there, and I became tired, hungry, and discouraged.

But as I walked across the canyon floor toward a shale ridge I intended to climb, miracle of miracles, I spotted a ram bedded right there on the floor at the head of the ravine. Even at that distance, I could see golden, heavy horns that flared outward at the tips. I immediately dropped to my belly, out of sight of the ram again, and slithered back in the direction from which I'd come. Once hidden behind the curve of the slope, I climbed up and toward the ram. The wind was negligible, the fine, black shale enabled me to stalk quietly, and everything seemed perfect. At last, I thought, a ram!

I eased around to where I could see the sheep less than a hundred yards away; he was still bedded staring away from me. His horns were massive, the weight carried well out toward the tips, and he was nearly as large as a caribou through the body. But rams normally live in bands, so I thought that there were probably others just around the little bend in the creek—maybe even that 43-incher I'd seen several years earlier. Though I had the cross hairs solid behind the ram's shoulder, I just had to find out if a bigger ram was just around the corner. Apparently, I didn't believe that a ram in the hand was worth two up the creek.

At that moment, the big ram jumped up and stared hard in my direction, then bounded for the shale slope. He trotted up it a few yards, then turned to stare. A moment later another ram trotted up beside him, but though he was a good full-curl trophy, he wasn't quite as big as the first ram. I put the cross hairs just behind the big one's shoulder as he trotted across the shale, and I pressed the trigger. At the muzzle blast, the ram turned abruptly, took a few steps back in the direction he'd come, and collapsed. He was the best ram I'd taken to that time. Approaching in the open where sheep have been shot at before seldom, if ever, works. But much of Dall sheep range is wilder-

Once rams accept you and you approach from below in the open, you can get very close.

ness, and sheep there aren't particularly worried about predators below them. They know that in the rocks they're safe from wolves and bears, and they haven't had experience with men with rifles. They probably view a man in the valley as just another wolf: He's nothing to worry about as long as they keep to the rocks and have a cliff or two handy to climb. Sheep are quick learners, though, and once they're shot at or have seen other rams shot, they won't make the same mistake. Sheep in parts of Montana, most of Alberta, and British Columbia hide in timber like deer and elk and will completely leave the area when badly frightened by man.

I'd learned while photographing sheep in Denali National Park that rams wouldn't run from me if I approached in the open and from below without making any attempt to sneak. Or at least some rams wouldn't. It had worked often enough for me that I had some faith in the tactic. If, on the other hand, I sneaked above the sheep without their knowledge, then peeped over a ridge and surprised them, they'd take off running and wouldn't stop until they were on the next mountain. A wolf above them is definitely bad news. So I approached from below and in the open, and most of the good photos I got were by using this tactic. I reasoned that since it had worked with a camera, it also should work with a rifle in a place this remote. And it does—sometimes.

17

Stone Sheep: British Columbia's Real Gold

Stone sheep inhabit typical sheep country—in other words spectacular regions. They feed in grassy slopes, tundra basins, and valley shin-
tangle, but always remain near cliffs as a means of escape should
predators threaten. Stone sheep are only found in northern British
Columbia, with the Peace River their southern boundary and the
rivers and lakes along the British Columbia-Yukon border their
northern.

Stone sheep behave just as Dalls and bighorns do. They rut in
November and December, they typically have several home ranges
during the year, and they express and seek dominance in the same
way. The biggest, and some argue the darkest, Stone sheep come
from the east slope of the Rockies. The famous Chadwick ram, which
has been on display for several years in the Buffalo Bill Museum in
Cody, Wyoming, is considered to be the top big-game head ever taken
in North America. According to the 1981 edition of *Records of North
American Big Game*, it was killed in the Muskwa River drainage on the
east slope of the Rockies. I've seen the mount—the fore half of a
sheep's body—a number of times, and I'm always astonished by its
size. The longest horn on the Chadwick ram is 51⁵/₈ inches; both

bases are 14⁶/₈ inches. If I ever manage to collect a ram even approaching that one, I think I'd retire from sheep hunting!

I'd hunted Dalls several times before I made my first Stone sheep hunt. I'd gone after the Dalls in the wild, remote, untouched north where the sheep had never seen a man. There, still hunting up canyons had been successful and it was also most natural, since I'd cut my teeth still hunting for mule deer in the Rockies. When I hunted Stone sheep in British Columbia with Ralph Kitchen, a guide for Folding Mountain Outfitters at the time, I learned about patience in stalking sheep. We did do some still hunting, and at that I felt very comfortable. But Ralph spent more time glassing than I normally did, and he was more thorough, combing every foot of ground in suspected sheep cover, gridding with binoculars or even spotting scope back and forth, searching crevasses, shadows, and tangles of short, stunted pine and spruce. The thorough glassing did pay off, since we spotted some forty rams in the six days of actual hunting we managed between rain and snow squalls, fog, and sleet. About six of those rams were legal, full-curl sheep (in British Columbia, 8½ years old). The rams ranged from black with white underparts to quite light in color with white heads and necks and gray saddles. I was color conscious here because I didn't want to shoot a ram that was so light as to be almost indistinguishable from Dall sheep mounts.

One day we still-hunted down the smooth, sloping back side of Corrugated Mountain, hoping to surprise a band of sheep that fed there. We walked downhill in the open. I didn't have much faith in the tactic, but it worked and we did catch the band of sheep. They'd winded us but couldn't quite figure out where we were, so they milled about in confusion. Ralph and I had blundered into them at close range, and when Ralph raised up from behind a small knoll to determine which was the best, his eyes nearly bugged out. I was behind a bush and couldn't see them, so he tried to explain to me which sheep to take while I tried to keep track of what he was saying. We didn't get that big ram, however, and later in the season it was collected by another hunter. It turned out to be a 42½-by-14½-inch ram that green-scored 176 Boone-and-Crockett points.

I won't relate the whole story here; basically, we spooked the sheep off the mountain. There turned out to be two monsters in the band. One of them was apparently very old; he either couldn't or wouldn't keep up with the rest and split off from the band as it headed up a canyon across the valley, climbed a scree slope, and eventually bedded at the base of a gray limestone cliff. After Ralph consoled me, we hiked into the valley bottom, crossed the creek,

Spectacular Stone sheep country in northern British Columbia.

climbed through thick tangles of willows and blown-down spruce, navigated a boulder slide, edged across a cliff, and worked to the bottom of the creek in the canyon where the big ram was—we hoped—still bedded. Up until that point in the long, arduous approach, we'd been completely hidden from the ram by the mountainside.

Ralph climbed a small rise very carefully and peeked over from behind a thick, stunted spruce tree. The ram was still there. We dropped down the slope, crossed a small meadow on our bellies, and slid down a small bluff on our pants seats to the creek. Then we stalked cautiously up the creek. Parts of it were hidden from the ram's field of view. But other places were in plain view of the ram, and there we had to be extremely careful, even though he was still more than half a mile away. Ralph had a great deal of respect for the ram's eyesight and cautiousness. These Stones were heavily hunted by men with long-range rifles.

And so the stalk went, until we were once more out of the ram's vision, hidden by the curve of the slope below him. The ram hadn't seemed suspicious when we'd last seen him, so there was every reason to hope he'd still be there after we eased up the rocky slope. My last glimpse of the sheep through the spotting scope told me that he was heavily broomed, massive, and old. He'd be an exceptional trophy, though not quite as good as the one that had gotten away earlier.

We walked slowly up the slope, then eased up the rock slide on hands and feet to be quiet. When we peeked over, the ram was gone. There was a cave and ledge farther up, and we hoped he'd gone into it. But he hadn't. While we were out of sight below, he had apparently either walked up the canyon or climbed the slope to the top of the cliffs and then gone into the next drainage. We did not find him again, and we didn't know whether he'd sensed us or just moved off on some errand of his own. It was not one of my best days: We'd failed on two tries at record-class rams.

The weather in the Toad River drainage can be unpredictable at best, and downright impossible at worst. Snow and rain kept us in our leaky, holey tent for several days (even in the tent, we slept under pack tarps), and then we were fogged in. Ralph kept telling me horror stories about clients who had been fogged in for their entire two-week hunt. Those tales made me extremely nervous, since I'd spent ten grand on the hunt and there'd be no telling when I could afford to do it again. When the weather cleared, we decided to try Ralph's sure thing, the Fish Bowl.

We saddled our horses and rode toward a high ridge we'd have to climb on foot to reach the Fish Bowl. The horses weren't too well broken to start with, and since ours was the first hunt of the season, they hadn't been ridden since the previous hunting season. They were skittish, unpredictable, and downright devilish. I wasn't paying as much attention to my horse as I should have been—I was busy scanning the peaks and ridges for sheep—and when I least expected it, the nag gave a heave and lunged, and I was suddenly sitting in the brush. My first and most satisfying inclination was to shoot the damned horse, but with great reluctance, I decided against it. In any case, I paid closer attention to that fiend the rest of the day.

We labored up a rock slide that led onto the plateau, then hiked across the flats to the rim of the Fish Bowl. I immediately found rams and mentally patted myself on the back as I directed Ralph to where they were bedded half a mile below. There were two good rams in the bunch, so we planned to sneak up on them. The first part of the sneak was easy. We simply backed up onto the plateau and walked along the

Stone rams near Muncho Lake, British Columbia.

flat. We then eased down a steep, jagged rockslide. Before long, we spooked a ram we hadn't seen, but he didn't act too alarmed and the rams below paid no attention. As we eased over the sharp, treacherous rock, we were careful not to rattle the loose scree. Sheep live in steep and rocky country where rocks and boulders are often just at the angle of repose. Pebbles, rocks, and boulders are constantly crashing down slopes, and aside from getting out of the way should it be necessary, sheep pay little attention. But if there are constant, small noises from a given direction, sheep become suspicious, especially if they've been shot at.

Stubby was in this group of rams, and he stood up and oriented himself in our direction before he bedded down again. Another big ram did the same. We crawled to the lip of a ledge and lay down to watch them, hoping their suspicions would subside. Thirty minutes later, we continued the stalk, trying to be silent. But that was impossible on the unstable, limestone rockslide. Finally, after at least three hours, we were getting close enough to begin thinking we might actually be successful. That was until Ralph, while crossing an avalanche chute, broke loose a refrigerator-size boulder and began sliding off on it. *Hell*, I thought, *that'll scare 'em for sure!* I sprinted across the steep chute, no longer paying attention to the rocks careening down the slide and nearly onto the sheep below. *Ralph could fend for himself*, I thought. *I want that ram!*

I ran to the edge of a cliff. The rams were up and milling, and one group had split off and was looking up cautiously at the falling rocks while walking quickly toward the valley floor, I suppose with the intention of climbing the opposite slope. Incredibly, one ram was still bedded straight below me at something over three hundred yards, and I believed he was the largest of the band. He had better than a full curl, the horn tips came up above the line of the snout, his horns were heavy and dark, and his cape was the darkest of any in the group. I made a quick decision, put the cross hairs low on the chest at the steep downhill angle, and pressed the trigger just as the ram stood and was about to plunge down the chute. He crumpled at the shot but bounced down the chute anyway, and then tumbled end over end for another four hundred yards. I thought he'd never stop falling, and I despaired for the horns.

He eventually rolled to a stop in the bottom of the canyon. He turned out to be quite a good ram, though nowhere near the class of those two old-timers I'd blown chances at a few days earlier. The horns were a very dark mahogany and as even as any I'd seen, they were heavy, and they curled in close to the face. Remarkably, they'd survived the tumble, though they were badly scratched up. I breathed a sigh of relief, too, because now I wouldn't have to keep a watchful eye on the weather all the time. In fact, at that point, I didn't give a damn what it did. Ralph and I celebrated back in the leaky tent that evening with a good, single-malt scotch I'd brought just for that occasion.

While hunting Stone sheep in the Toad River country, I'd noticed that they often fed lower in the valleys and in more gentle country than Dall sheep normally do. This is probably because there are fewer wolves, at least in some Stone sheep country. (I didn't see a fresh wolf track or even hear one howl while I was there, unlike all Dall sheep country I've been in.) As a result, sheep are less fearful and more apt to venture into the lush grazing of valley bottoms. I've also noticed that when browsing in valley bottoms, Stone sheep use their noses more than Dall sheep in the Alaska Range do, and from time to time they'd raise their noses into the wind and test it for danger. Stalking and approaching Stone sheep in gentler country requires staying out

Stone sheep country on the Toad River. I killed my first Stone ram about ten miles behind the mountain on the right.

of sight *and* keeping downwind. I don't really know how keenly they scent, but certainly not as well as bears, mule deer, moose, or elk.

I'm told that Stone sheep on the Spatsizi Plateau feed in rolling and fairly gentle tundra and grasslands on top of the plateau and rely heavily on scent to detect danger. Sheep outfitters in the place typically take wind direction into account when stalking. For the most part, though, sheep guides and hunters don't worry much about wind direction until they're fairly close to rams.

Which leads me to another important point. When stalking sheep, or any game, for that matter, it's important to take into account the wind direction where the quarry is, not where you are, unless you're close. The direction grass or weeds are bending, the pattern of ruffling fur, and the direction perching birds are facing (they invariably face into the wind) are a few of the clues to wind direction where the animal is bedding or feeding. I once collected a nice ram just because I paid attention to the direction some fine, wispy snow was blowing over a ridge near where he was bedded. I stalked into the wind and out of sight, and shot the ram at about twenty yards.

Typical British Columbia Stone sheep country is mostly straight up and down, and it's spectacular enough to take your breath away. The odds of collecting a trophy ram with most outfitters are good— many are running 100 percent success on ram quotas varying from three to sixteen per season—and there are few trophies as unique and impressive as a big Stone ram, even if he isn't the Chadwick. Unfortunately, good two-week Stone sheep hunts start at around ten thousand U.S. dollars, making this one of the most expensive species on the continent to hunt. In spite of that, I hope I haven't made my last Stone sheep hunt yet.

18

Bighorn Sheep

Bighorns live farther south than Dalls and Stones and consequently closer to human population centers. Bighorns live in the Rocky Mountains as far north as Jasper, Alberta, (at roughly the same latitude as Edmonton), and I'm told that some populations go even a bit farther north around Prince George, British Columbia. Generally, bighorns have had more experience with men with rifles than have thinhorn mountain sheep, so many of them have learned to hide in timber as do mule deer and elk. But they rut, seek and express dominance, and migrate in much the same way as the sheep of the Far North.

Rocky Mountain bighorn sheep populations in huntable numbers range from Colorado on the south, through western Wyoming, Montana, Idaho, Oregon, and Washington, to British Columbia as far north as the central part of the province and to Alberta on the east slope of the Rockies.

In the past, many of the biggest heads were taken out of the Alberta Rockies, but few exceptional sheep are killed there nowadays, even though there are a number of outfitters with ram quotas in the mountains surrounding Banff and Jasper National Parks. Canadian acquaintances have told me that large rams aren't killed there anymore mostly because of resident hunting pressure. I'd considered making an Alberta bighorn hunt, but I talked with more than two dozen references who'd hunted with at least five outfitters, and I got the same story over and over: The sheep mountains were overrun with resident hunters who were constantly interfering with stalks and bringing ATVs into sheep country, and big rams just no longer existed. No one had even seen a ram in the 170-point class, and many hunters went away without a shot. Others took small sheep, but nothing to write home about. If I'm paying ten to fifteen grand for a sheep, I want to at least enjoy the solitude, which seems to be a thing of the past in Alberta sheep country. For the money, I'd rather go on another Stone sheep hunt in northern British Columbia. The odds are much better, the sheep bigger, the country less crowded and spoiled, and you're not as likely to run into that bane of all wild-country hunting, the ATV.

The best bets for a really large bighorn ram seem to be in the drawing areas of Montana, such as the Sun River country and some areas around Butte. I've seen several heads brought into various taxidermists with 17-inch-plus bases and Boone-and-Crockett scores between 195 and 201. Many were relatively young rams. The odds are long against drawing a permit for these areas, however. Another good bet, though the rams don't get nearly as big there, is the country around Cody, Wyoming, much of which borders Yellowstone National Park just to the west. The odds in most areas there are about twenty to one against drawing a permit, but if you do get one and you hunt with a reputable guide, success is high—around 100 percent—and some rams are quite good. I know of at least one 42-inch ram taken that had heavy bases, though not quite like those 17-plus-inchers.

I hunted bighorns in southern Montana in what were then called "open areas," which meant that anyone who cared to buy a permit could hunt bighorn sheep. I hunted without a guide in the Absaroka-Beartooth Wilderness just north of Yellowstone, and I had good success with elk and deer, but not with sheep. I'd talked with state biologists beforehand, had narrowed down places to look, and had spent weeks on preseason scouting. I had located several bands with legal three-quarter-curl rams, but none in my opinion were worth shooting, so I passed them by. In those areas, the season is closed as soon as one or two sheep are taken. I have a friend from New England who had booked a hunt for sheep in one of those open areas, but by the time he arrived in Montana, the hunt was over because the area's sheep limit had already been reached.

The younger legal rams I saw on those hunts stayed to the timber.

They favored rocky outcrops or cliffs that jutted from big stands of lodgepole pines. From these perches, sheep could spot hunters across the canyon or along the creekbottom, then disappear among the trees. Hunting them was frustrating if you employed the methods used for Dalls and Stones in the Far North. Several times I located bands of young rams, but usually there was none over seven years old in the group. Just as often, even though I thought I was hidden in the trees as I glassed them, they would also locate me and then file off the rock outcrop to disappear in the timber. Fortunately I could track, and that's what I did.

I followed their deer-sized hoofprints through the pine-needle duff for hours. This kind of hunting resembled tracking wise old mule deer bucks in timber, and I found myself testing the wind and watching on the downwind side of the trail just as I would for a bedded buck. Eventually I caught up with the sheep. They were climbing a shale ridge on the far side of Flood Creek two hundred or so yards away, within comfortable rifle range. I glassed them carefully, and two rams definitely exceeded the three-quarter-curl minimum, but they just weren't trophies. I let them go, hoping to eventually find a bigger ram. I didn't, however, and after my second hunt in that region, I realized that there probably were no real trophy rams in those open areas.

I'm told by several outfitters in northwestern Wyoming that bighorns there don't behave quite so much like deer—in other words, hunting them involves more glassing, more long stalks, and less tracking. But at times, bighorn sheep in these areas still do behave like deer or elk in the timber, something I've never witnessed among Dall sheep. Again, part of the reason for this is that in more southern climes, man has harried sheep mercilessly for more than a century now, while the northern Stones and Dalls have been only lightly hunted in most places. Also, there are now no wolves on bighorn ranges in Montana and Wyoming, yet wolves are abundant in Dall sheep country, which I believe causes sheep there to be afraid to go into the trees. I've observed this in the Wrangells, Alaska, and Brooks ranges. In many far north Dall sheep ranges, with all the wolves around, venturing into the timber or lowlands would be tantamount to suicide for a sheep.

For now, I don't plan to hunt bighorns unless I can draw a permit in one of the top Wyoming or Montana areas. I've been putting in for drawings in Wyoming off and on for a dozen years, and perhaps half as much in Montana. I've yet to draw a permit, but it's nice to think that the odds might start tipping in my favor, though I know this is not really how the laws of probability work.

California bighorns are a smaller variety of bighorn and are most abundant in southern British Columbia. On a recent hunt there with Ken Olynyk, we normally spotted more than a hundred sheep a day, with at least ten of these rams over two years of age. In spite of those numbers, however, few rams reached or exceeded the three-quarters curl that was legal. Early in the hunt, I did pass up several barely legal three-quarter curl rams. By the tail end of the hunt, I was feeling desperate. We hadn't seen anything of trophy size, hunting pressure was as heavy as a New York deer opening, the weather was hot and dry, and I was wishing I'd never heard of the place.

After going to a supposed hot spot early before dawn and finding six other hunters there, I decided we should hunt elsewhere. After a three-hour drive and an hour hike, we were glassing across a steep gorge at a band of six rams, two of them real trophies and by far the biggest we'd seen in nine days of hunting. We planned for Ken and Calvin, an assistant guide, to stay put and direct me as I made the stalk. If the rams moved off, they'd signal the direction; if they bedded, they'd fold their hands against their heads as if they were going to sleep, and so on. I slid down the incredibly steep mountain for thirty minutes and climbed up the equally steep opposite slope, around the shoulder of the mountain from the bedded rams. I was nearly to the place we'd decided I'd shoot from, when Ken or Calvin (it was too far to tell for sure which) began signaling that the rams had moved off to the right. (At this point, the guides hadn't seen me, but were just signaling.) I took this to mean the sheep were *really* moving, so I headed down the slope and across the immense slide where the sheep had been bedded. Actually, the sheep had only moved a few yards and bedded again, and I'd have been within easy rifle range at the point where I had originally planned a shot. As it worked out, I stalked across the noisy, rocky slide to within two hundred yards of the sheep, but I couldn't see them since they were above me. Eventually they caught my scent and filed over the mountain. We resolved to make better plans the next time.

Ken and I were back the next morning. I spotted two rams feeding into timber far up the valley, and Ken spotted a lone ram on the rockslide across the canyon. We attempted to refine our prearranged signals, and I set off again. The ram was definitely not a big one, but it *was* my last day, so I took out after him. I climbed into the bottoms and started up a hidden cliff in the center of the rockslide. I got above where the ram had been, watching for Ken's signals. He didn't signal, which meant the ram was still bedded. The day was warming, the air becoming less dense and drifting uphill, so I had to get above the ram and stalk down on him or he'd scent me before I could shoot. I did get above and eased down to where I thought he was bedded. He wasn't there, and I became a bit confused; things looked so different on this side of the canyon. Finally Ken began to signal. I was looking up at him and into the sun, so it was tough to tell just what he was trying to say. Finally, I thought he pointed down, and then made a small gesture with his hands, which I took to mean the ram was a short distance below (at least I read this correctly). I eased down the slope, peered over a scrubby juniper, and the ram was staring at me less than thirty yards away. One bullet settled him, and he crashed down the slope and into the timber below. As it turned out, Ken didn't even see me stalking across the slope until I was within forty yards of the ram, and he was astonished I'd gotten so close. The ram was a bit better than the legal three-quarter curl. No whopper, but like so many other trophies, I *really* value him for that unique stalk.

19

Desert Bighorns: Toughest of the Grand Slam

Desert bighorns are the most difficult of the four varieties of North American sheep to collect. This is because it's very tough to secure a permit. Arizona has a number of areas where sheep hunting is allowed. The odds are best in certain areas in the south of the state; there they are about fifty to one against drawing a permit. In other areas, the odds are even worse, possibly one hundred to one against drawing. I've been applying for the eight-hundred-dollar permit for a decade, now, without luck.

Desert sheep can also be hunted on the Hualapai Indian Reservation in Arizona just adjacent to Grand Canyon National Park. Hunts there were going for about twenty grand the last time I checked, but as a tribal representative told me in 1989, you hunt until you get one and success is virtually 100 percent. I've been seriously considering that hunt, even though the rams aren't particularly large, but it's hard to justify plunking down twenty thousand dollars for a hunt for just one animal. For that price, you could make a reasonably good African safari and take maybe ten trophies. I guess it depends on your priorities, and sheep hunters (myself included) are a strange and foolish lot, or they wouldn't pay such prices.

Mexico, too, now has drawings for sheep permits. The odds are considerably better, though I've heard some horror stories about Mexican sheep hunts. Most, if not all, nonresident sheep hunting is conducted in the mountains of Baja. I haven't yet applied for a Mexican desert sheep permit, but I'm thinking hard about it.

Desert sheep inhabit mountain ranges, usually volcanic in origin, where vegetation is scarce, spiny, or poisonous and where visibility is good. They rely almost exclusively on vision to detect danger, and then climbing and running to escape it. If a good ram spots you in Mexico, where sheep are often hunted illegally by locals, he will take off. It's critical to keep out of sight on the stalk. I've stalked desert sheep off and on for twenty years in order to photograph them. I've done so chiefly in southern Arizona in places where they're protected and never hunted, such as Organ Pipe National Monument. They're consequently less spooky, though it's still no cinch to sneak up on one. I've also waited in rock blinds or hides beside *tanques* (springs or seeps, usually dammed up by man to create a basin) in the Cabeza Prieta and Kofa National Wildlife Refuges, and I've stalked them in the Sierra Viejo of Sonora, Mexico. Over the years, I've managed to get a few close-ups of good rams, but considering the number of years I've spent doing it, the results haven't been spectacular.

I once spent nearly two weeks backpacking through the Pinacate Mountains north and west of Puerto Penasco, Sonora, looking for rams that were said to live in some volcanic craters there. All I came away with were some photos of tracks. That seems to be my story with desert sheep: I keep applying for a hunting permit without success, and I keep trying to get a spectacular photo of a big desert ram, also mostly without success. I have seen some record-class heads in southern Arizona, though, and I even have a mediocre photo of a ram that would probably be record-book material.

When after desert sheep, hunters usually glass and then plan what is often a long and arduous approach. Sometimes they ambush the sheep at *tanques* when they come to drink. Since there's typically little vegetation in desert sheep country, stalking desert sheep is a bit like stalking Dall sheep north of the Arctic Circle, and keeping out of sight on the approach involves staying behind ridges or mountains or hiding in arroyos until you're within rifle range. Sheep are not tracked in far north mountain ranges, because the tundra is springy and doesn't take a hoofprint and because of rocks. Sheep in southern ranges are seldom tracked but it is a possibility there since sand will hold prints, and a couple of hunters have told me they've done so.

Until I collect a decent desert ram, I will continue to apply for a permit in Arizona and to consider the other options of Mexico and the Hualapai Indian Reservation. Someday I hope to secure a desert bighorn trophy.

20

The Mountain Goat: King of the Crags

The Rocky Mountain goat lives in the most rugged country on the planet. It presses hard against the outer limits of mammalian survival, living comfortably on the bare faces of sheer cliffs through storms and winds that would topple a man. I've seen goats at cliff bases along the Gulf of Alaska seashore, and I've seen them at higher than twelve thousand feet above sea level in the Montana Rockies.

Mountain goats were probably first described in the early nineteenth century by Lewis and Clark. They thought that the Rocky Mountain goat was a variety of mountain sheep, probably beginning the confusion between the two that continues today. More than once I've heard tourists in Yellowstone or Glacier National Park call a bighorn sheep a mountain goat.

Mountain goats are able to eat and metabolize a wide variety of plants. They graze on the scant grasses and lichens that get a foothold in nooks on the sheer faces of granite or limestone walls, they eat conifer saplings, and they nibble at willows, moss, wildflowers, and poplars.

Whereas sheep in very rough country bounce from foothold to foothold, often seeming to run down cliff faces, goats are slow and deliberate scalers. They won't hurry down a cliff or very steep slope unless they've lost their balance. They often plant their backsides firmly against a slope or a cliff as they descend slowly. In this manner, goats are able to go places that would kill a mountain sheep. One benefit of being able to climb into country that is inaccessible to other game species is that there's little competition for food. At the same time, goats also have the option of moving down in altitude if necessary because of bad weather. Goats frequently winter at the same altitude at which mountain sheep and mule deer summer, and then the goats summer much higher.

Female, or nanny, goats may have horns just as long as males'. On my first goat hunt in British Columbia's Cariboo Plateau country, in the mid-1960s, a hunter killed an 11-inch female. The horns were much thinner than a male's would be, but they were good enough to be listed in the Boone-and-Crockett record book. Later in that hunt, I killed two goats, which was the limit then. The larger was a 10-inch, ten-year-old billy. I compared the horns of that billy with those of the big nanny. The bases of the billy's horns measured 5½ inches in circumference, and the nanny's a bit under 4 inches. The billy's horns tapered smoothly from base to tip, and the distance between horn bases was narrower by a bit over an inch. In comparison with the body, the horns of billies are proportionately smaller than those of mature nannies, because a billy has a much larger body size.

On that hunt, we climbed through hip-deep wet snow in late November to get a good goat. It was extremely dangerous hunting, since the new, heavy, wet snow in that steep country was just looking for an excuse to break free in an avalanche. I stood in the predawn darkness while Herbie, my Shuswap guide, filled the horses' grain bags. Avalanches periodically broke free farther up the canyon, with the rumble of distant artillery fire, then rolled down avalanche channels. I wasn't looking forward to stalking goats in that, and Herbie was even more reluctant. But we went anyway.

Goats, like mountain sheep and mule deer above timberline, rely primarily on vision to find danger and on climbing into inaccessible country to escape it. Therefore, stalking goats involves staying out of sight. The first step is to trek or pack into known goat country. Then you need to glass thoroughly. It's tough to spot the white goats from a distance against snow, and even more so for the neophyte. It took me several days of glassing before I was able to find goats on snow. Eventually I began to notice things such as shadows and the tiny black slivers of horns. Also, the goat's coat was the color of light cream, while the snow was that of the best typing paper.

Herbie and I would start the day by glassing the cliffs and ledges above us as soon as it got light. More often than not, we found goat trails in the heavy snow. Since it was snowing almost every night, we knew the trails were fresh. We'd then climb up to the trails and glass again from there. We found plenty of goats, but getting up on them was another matter. These goats had been hunted and knew just what a man looked like and represented. As soon as they saw a human, they'd head up the face of a sheer limestone wall or over the ridge in their calm, methodical manner. We just didn't have the energy to fight our way through the heavy, hip-deep snow in pursuit of the goats. We didn't have white clothing for camouflage, which would have helped, so we found it absolutely necessary to stay out of sight until close enough to shoot. That wasn't always easy, either. If there wasn't a ravine or ridge between us and a billy, we simply gave that one up and looked for another.

We finally found a herd of billies browsing on stunted, wind-tortured spruce in a gully near the top of the plateau. We climbed up through the snow and cliffs, our hearts often in our throats because of the precarious positions we'd find ourselves in. We got to within three hundred yards of the goats; fortunately, they were still in the same place. I picked out one of the biggest goats and put the cross hairs between his shoulder blades as he climbed out of the ravine opposite me. Just as the goat took a jump, I pressed the trigger. The bullet hit too far back, angling forward just behind the rib cage. The billy took a couple of quick hops, then climbed over the ridge as I tried to get another shot. We picked up the blood trail on top and followed. I was eighteen at the time, young, strong, and with no idea about pacing myself. Before long I'd left Herbie behind as I trailed the billy.

Twice I'd seen the goat below as we walked through the skeletons of a burned-over forest, but I hadn't been able to get a shot. Hours later, I eased over a ridge and down into a steep avalanche chute. I was feeling the strain of forcing my way through waist-deep snow, and I breathed a silent prayer of thanks when I saw the billy standing on a ledge on the other side. I settled the cross hairs of the 7mm Magnum on his shoulders and tried to still my heart, which was pounding from the exertion and excitement and was making the cross hairs dance like a seismograph needle on the slopes of Vesuvius. When it did finally ease, I touched the trigger. The goat hunched, folded, tumbled off the ledge, and then wedged between two charred spruce trunks on the ledge below.

I was trying to figure out how to get at the goat on the ledge, when I saw a movement just below. A big billy stepped from behind a drift and turned to look. There was blood on his long, shaggy white fur; he was the one I'd been tracking. I'd just killed a different, uninjured, billy—it was lucky that British Columbia allowed two goats. I put the cross hairs behind his shoulder as he started down into the chute, then pulled the trigger. He rolled over into the chute and a moment later climbed out of it on the other side. I fired again and he sagged, but then he got his feet under him and continued up. I shot once more, aiming for the base of the neck, and he collapsed, bounced down the ledges in a gathering cloud of fine snow, and then went into and down the chute. I ran to the edge and looked over. I traced his progress by the rising cloud of snow; minutes later he was bouncing through snow-covered boulders at the base of the cliffs two thousand feet below. I despaired of seeing the horns in one piece.

I worked my way cautiously up the cliff, sweat trickling down my forehead in spite of subfreezing temperatures, to free the goat on the ledge. He was a good one, too, though not quite as good as the other. I freed him and shoved him off the ledge and into the chute. He followed the other billy's route down into the bottom of the canyon. As I eased down into the chute and started across it to find a way into the gorge, the heavy snow and ice gave way with a crack like a pistol shot, and I rocketed down the chute and over a ledge atop tons of snow and ice. I wound up in the tops of a tangle of spruce saplings as the rest of the avalanche rumbled by into the gorge. My hands get clammy whenever I recall that one, even today, twenty-five years later.

Herbie showed up shortly thereafter. We both reconnoitered the terrain and found that the avalanche chute was the only way to get through and below the towering cliffs to the goats. Dangerous though it was, we really had no other choice. As it turned out, it wasn't really as bad as we'd feared; the avalanche I'd broken loose earlier had cleared out most of the loose snow and ice.

We found the goats within a few yards of each other. The horns of the bigger goat were still intact, but unfortunately, the smaller had had one horn broken off in the two-thousand-foot fall. Incredibly, the larger goat—with five bullets through the lungs, shoulders, and neck, and a broken back from that long fall—was still alive. I have no doubt that a four-hundred-pound billy goat is the toughest animal on the continent. The smaller of the two goats measured 9½ inches with 5-inch bases, and the big one 10 inches with 5½-inch bases. I'm convinced that goat hunting is every bit as dangerous as hunting grizzlies, if not more so.

Goats are confident in their ability to escape predators, including man, and in lightly hunted or unhunted country, they'll often let you approach well within rifle range before they think it's time to climb into the cliffs. By then it's too late for them, if you have a rifle and want to use it. But in more accessible areas along Alaska's southern coast or in central and coastal British Columbia, goats know what a man means and stay out of rifle range. There, as when I hunted those goats in the sixties, it's necessary to stay hidden until you're ready to shoot. Goats don't have the reputation for keen eyesight that mountain sheep do, but in my experience, they see just as well.

The goat is not at the top of the list of North American big game. A goat isn't the trophy that a good ram is; its horns aren't as long, massive, or impressive, and even a 10-inch billy can't measure up to a mature Stone ram. Of those who haven't hunted for trophy goats, almost no one notices the 10-inch billy I have hanging in my trophy room. Instead, they're drawn to the mountain sheep, Cape buffalo, leopard, kudu, or moose heads. Only those who have hunted goats before appreciate that old billy. They know what you have to go through to get one. Because goats live in dangerous country, a hunter must have the lungs of a decathlete, the nerves of a bullfighter, and the legs of a distance runner to hunt them comfortably. The rest of us must just tolerate the pain in order to hunt them, or give up on mountain goats completely.

21

The Grizzly: North America's Most Dangerous Game

The grizzly bear is considered North America's most dangerous animal, though I believe that hunting mountain goats and mountain sheep can at times be more dangerous. Grizzlies, like mule deer, occupy a variety of habitat types, from beaches along the British Columbia coast to some of the thickest and densest forests on the continent, to vast barren tundra plains, even up to well above timberline in open basins and on plateaus. I've photographed the big, unpredictable, shaggy bears in all habitats, but I prefer stalking them in the mountains above timberline. Part of the reason is why I also find sheep hunting so attractive: It's the closest I'm likely to get to heaven. Too, you can glass and locate a bear from some distance away and then carefully plan your stalk. Because of the open terrain, it can be classic stalking at its finest: a well-planned approach on a potentially dangerous animal.

Grizzlies inhabit above-timberline mountains in any part of their range where peaks occur. I've watched bears grazing on lush late-spring and summer herbage in Yellowstone, the Bob Marshall Wilderness in Montana, and Banff National Park in Alberta. I've seen them above timberline in the Alaska, Brooks, and Wrangell ranges in Alaska, and I've hunted them above timberline with both gun and camera.

In most of the Brooks that I'm familiar with, grizzlies spend the majority of their time high. That far north, grizzlies come out of hibernation anywhere from early April, if there's been a mild winter and an early spring, to mid-May, if the snows have been heavy during winter and the temperatures low. Farther south, grizzlies emerge from hibernation earlier, depending on factors such as altitude, the severity of the winter, and temperature. I've seen bears just out of winter dens in March in Montana's Absaroka-Beartooth Wilderness. Normally, bears have thick, glossy coats when they first come out of hibernation, and spring bears always have better pelts than autumn bears. If you're after a particularly fine bear rug, spring is the time to hunt.

Once the bears come out of hibernation, they head for the river-bottoms, where some grasses, sedges, and other edible plants such as peavine or saxifrage are already growing. As the days warm, they move higher and higher, following the newly sprouting plants all the way up, until by July they're nearly at the limit of plant growth. They usually stay high, too, and eat the emerging berries, grasses, and other vegetation that grow along the rocky creeks and ravines. They feast with relish on any carrion they can find; they'll clean up old wolf- or winter-killed caribou, moose, or mountain sheep that are being exposed by melting snows (and up in the very far north snow may still be melting in early August).

Bears will eat meat whenever they can get it, but they feed mostly on vegetation through the summer and fall. Those grizzlies that live in salmon country are the exception: They get meat and protein for much of the summer and into the fall, and they consequently grow much larger because of it. Those behemoth, ten-foot-plus brown bears of coastal Alaska are simply fish-fed grizzlies. Interior and far-north bears never get that big because they get little meat protein, so in those areas a bear that squares seven feet is as good as you can reasonably hope for, especially north of the Arctic Circle.

Bears eat during the summer. And eat. And eat. Their entire energies are directed toward putting on as much fat as they can before they go into hibernation again. Generally, the highest quality forage is that which is growing vigorously. During the summer, plants generally are growing fastest in high country, because there they have less time to complete growth and produce seeds before winter than they would in low country.

Bears in some places may stay in high basins all summer and well into the autumn. Many do so in the Far North, where hunting seasons open in early September. Unless there's been a very early and heavy snowfall, you'll find many up high; it's almost a sure wager that you'll get a good specimen if you hunt in the peaks until the first significant snowfall.

My favorite method of hunting high-country grizzlies is to simply find a good vantage point overlooking a lot of country. Since there is no forest or even very high brush there, a foraging bear will stick out like a cold sore at the prom. I know of one place where I can be assured of seeing three bears a day while just sitting and enjoying the view. Bears there graze up and down the valley along the benches for blueberries. And wolves often kill migrating caribou in the valley. If you find a wolf kill, that's a good place to ambush a bear, even if there isn't much meat left; bears will investigate any enticing scent and within a day or two will find what's left of the carcass.

In these regions it's hard to get an accurate idea of just how big a given grizzly really is. There are no large trees anywhere around and the bears all look immense when compared with the scrubby, two-foot dwarf birch or eight-inch lowbush blueberry plants. I've found that a bear is usually a big one if his head appears small in proportion to his body. A number of bear-hunting guides with more experience than I have agree. To be able to recognize a small-headed bear, though, you have to compare a lot of bears. Most won't be trophy class—that is, they'll appear large-headed.

When you've found a grizzly whose head seems small in proportion to his body, plan your stalk carefully. Bears have as keen a sense of smell as any animal I've hunted, so don't approach from upwind. As an illustration of how keen a grizzly's sense of smell really is, consider this: A bear once scented our two-day-old trail across the tundra. I was resting on a high shale ridge after an unsuccessful stalk for sheep. A blond grizzly ambled along far below near where we'd backpacked into the country two days before. The bear stopped just where we'd sat down to rest and pondered our scent seriously. And this was even after a rain the day before! So never underestimate a bear's nose.

Bears also have very good hearing. If you're getting close and the terrain you're stalking across is noisy, move only when the bear is stripping leaves from a bush or chewing (since a grizzly is an eating machine, he'll be doing this most of the time); that way his eating noises will mask the sounds you make as you get near.

Next time you see a grizzly rug, examine its eyes. Notice how small they are in proportion to the rest of the head. This indicates something about a grizzly's eyesight: It's not in the class with that of pronghorn antelope, mule deer, or mountain sheep. It's been fashionable for outdoor writers to talk about how poorly grizzlies see, but don't believe all of it. I've had bears see me at more than 400 yards in belly-deep dwarf birch or scrub willows. I once observed a sow and two yearling cubs watch a caribou give birth at least 450 yards away, then rush them and eat the calf. A grizzly is definitely sensitive to movement, even if he doesn't see quite as well as a mountain ram.

When stalking high-country grizzlies, plan your route fastidiously. Plan to stay downwind of the bear, or nearly so; watch for indications of wind direction where the bear is, such as the pattern of wind-blown fur or the direction grasses or shrubs are bending. Watch also for the consistency of the wind direction. If it's shifty and unreliable, you have your work cut out for you, and you'll also have to rely more heavily on luck. If the wind direction is shifting, try to pick the route that is least likely to be given away.

I once stalked an old, big, and very blond grizzly well above timberline. He was grazing up the canyon, thoroughly working over berry patches as he moved. The wind was blowing predominantly up the canyon. It was afternoon and the air was warming, becoming less dense, and rising up the hills. But the wind was also shifty, at times blowing in the opposite direction, down the canyon, and at other times blowing away from the cliffs the bear was paralleling. It seemed as though the best approach would be from the creekside, which was the only direction the wind didn't seem to blow. If I headed off on a tangent slightly up the canyon and toward the cliff, I should be okay. It almost worked, too, except that during the last stages of that stalk, I ran out of cover more than three hundred yards from the bear. I had enough respect for a bear's vision on that short, open tundra to know that he'd spot me if I tried to cross it. As luck would have it, the wind then shifted again, fanning my sweaty back, and within a few moments the bear had swapped ends and was chugging down the canyon.

The rougher the country, the easier it is to stay out of sight on the stalk. Since grizzlies almost always seem to be going somewhere, it's often possible to plan a stalk so that in the end the bear moves in to you. This is only possible, however, if the wind is blowing more or less from the bear to your ambush spot.

Several times I've stalked mountain grizzlies by approaching an animal carcass. Once I was hunting in a long valley through which caribou were migrating. They were everywhere, and wolves were living in predator heaven. Caribou were so abundant that wolves ate only a bit off the shoulders and hind legs, then moved on. This left a lot of grizzly feed around. In some mysterious manner, the abundance of caribou had been communicated to bears in other places, and almost overnight the valley had filled with shaggy, unpredictable grizzlies. One morning, as I squatted by the bush that served as an outhouse and stared out across the basin in reverie, a young bear stood abruptly on hind legs and *woofed*. I had about five years of life frightened out of me!

A couple of days earlier, I'd watched two wolves pull down a bull caribou half a mile from my tent. They'd fed only lightly on the carcass, and I was surprised that a bear hadn't already found it. The bull was large and promised an abundant supply of protein to any bear that stumbled upon it. I'd been stalking the carcass since the wolves had killed it, then hiding in thigh-high dwarf birch on a rise sixty yards away. I planned to do the same that day, too. I approached the carcass after circling to get downwind of it, moving slowly and quietly in a half crouch to keep a low profile. When I climbed the rise, there was no bear there, so I settled myself in and scrunched down into the brush to get out of the wind. Within two hours, a grizzly with a very black face and very blond shoulders showed up. He'd caught the scent of the meat at least a mile down the creek and followed it to the carcass the way a great white shark would zero in on blood in the sea. The rest was anticlimactic.

Stalking known feeding areas can also work well. There's a sloping foothill thick with lowbush blueberries at the base of a high peak. Traditionally, a big male owns that flat, and if another bear gets into it, he's in trouble. Since the flat is so thick with berries most years, that old male has a hard time keeping others out. Those berries are just too tempting to other bears, except mothers with young cubs, so they're always raiding it. Berries are at their best there in late August and early September, and since bear season opens September 1, it's one of the best places to stalk.

The place is very open, and there's little cover for concealment. During the day, heated air normally rises up the slope, so stalking from below doesn't work. I'd found that the best way to stalk the berry patch is to do it from below early in the morning while the air is still cool, dense, and flowing downhill. I'd walk to within half a mile of the flat and hurry up a small ravine that's just adequate to hide me if I half crouch my way up it; then I'd get on the uphill side of the patch just as the air began to heat and blow uphill. I could wait there all day for a bear without one ever sensing me. One September day I saw four different bears in that patch of blueberries, and that's a lot of grizzlies for that country.

Another reason I prefer hunting grizzlies above timberline in open country is that there you're far less likely to blunder into a bear at close range. Twice I've been chased or charged by bears I'd surprised in timber along salmon rivers. Once I was unarmed and barely escaped by leaping off a bluff onto my raft below. In grizzly country, especially if the salmon are running, I'm always a bit on edge when hiking through timber or brush, since I can't see far ahead. In the mountains above timberline, though, I can rely on my eyes to keep me out of trouble with bears, and I can find them at great distances if that's what I want. Being in mountain grizzly country, too, is at least as attractive as actually shooting a bear.

22

High-Country Wapiti

In many western states, the archery elk hunt is held early, sometimes as early as August. At that time, bands of bull elk, or wapiti, are frequently high and often above timberline. Even during the earliest rifle hunts, which usually open around mid-September, bull elk can be high, especially if it's hot and dry.

In Montana's Absaroka-Beartooth Wilderness, bulls will feed on the nearly ten-thousand-foot Buffalo Plateau and down into the basins on either side. At the bottoms of the basins there is thick lodgepole pine timber. In the morning, bulls will often feed down from the plateau top and basins and into the timber to bed for the day in its cool shade; then they'll feed back out into the basins and onto the plateau in the late afternoon. If the bugs are bad, bulls will bed instead on the open tops of plateaus or on ridges in the wind.

When hunting for most high-country bulls during the early seasons, it's best to ambush them as they feed out of the forest in the late afternoon or evening or when they feed back into the timber in the morning. It's probably even better to glass for bulls on the shady, north-facing slopes of the basins or on windy ridges, and then pull off a classic sneak.

If bulls are bedded on a windy plateau top, sneaking up on them is still possible. There are often small ravines, rocky outcrops, and other breaks in the terrain that will provide stalking cover. If they are bedded at the base of big rockslides on the north-facing side of basins, however, the approach can be more difficult. The cliffs are generally too high and steep for you to move down on them from above. It's sometimes possible to approach from one side or the other at about the same level as the bedded bulls, using rocks and rises for cover. Approaching from below doesn't normally work because during the day, when you will make most of your stalks, the air is warming and rising. But if a storm front is coming or passing through, bringing with it cool air, you can approach from below and still be stalking into the wind because the cold air is more dense and descends downhill. Usually, though, elk won't bed on shady north-facing slopes when it's cool, anyway.

One problem with hunting elk in high country early in the season, around the middle of September, is that the rut is just beginning. As a wildlife biologist, I did research on rutting behavior in elk and found that the peak of rutting activity on the average is around September 22. If it's been cold and stormy, however, elk may be rutting completely by mid-September, or if it's hot and dry, the rut may be set back a few days or even weeks.

One problem with hunting during the rut is that bull elk may suddenly move out of high basins to find cows at lower elevations, although if cows are using the same basins, the bulls will stay around. Those basins off Buffalo Plateau are mostly bull pastures, so bulls must leave them and go elsewhere to find the ladies. Just the same, at least some bulls hang back in the high country until the rut is fully under way late in September. And by then, it's a good possibility that the highest country is already snowed under. When I've hunted early season elk along Buffalo Plateau, I've stayed high as long as the weather would allow it and have killed bulls well above nine thousand feet from mid to late September. Often, too, there was snow on the ground, and when there is snow, tracking is an excellent tactic. If it's cold and bulls are still high, they bed in the upper reaches of timber at the bottoms of open basins, and then feed out into those basins until the snow gets so heavy that they can't get at the grasses and herbage.

Once I followed some tracks into a heavy stand of lodgepole pines in Telephone Basin. The bulls had been out feeding through about a foot of snow and probably just after daylight had fed back into the trees. There was a warm, northern chinook blowing, and the snow was rapidly melting. The tracks were softening and losing their sharp outlines, and this, along with snow that was melting and dropping from the timber onto the trail, made the tracks look older than they really were. I figured the tracks were quite old, when in truth they'd been made less than an hour earlier. So I was a bit careless as I trailed along, even though I did keep aware of wind direction. As a result, I blundered into the band of bulls in the trees at close range. Bulls were flying in every direction as I tried to pick out a good one for a shot. But they were gone in a moment.

I'd glimpsed at least six bulls, from yearlings up to a fair-sized 5 by 5. I followed the biggest track as it headed down into a thicker stand of timber and then up the canyon. But unfortunately, the bull was moving uphill and downwind with the warming and rising air; he'd scent me if I followed his trail as it was going, and then I would never see him again. The tracks showed that the bull was only walking, so he wasn't too frightened and would probably eventually stop and bed down again. The wind had been from the bulls to me when I jumped them, so they hadn't been able to smell me and probably didn't know what they were running from. I knew that the timber would peter out in the open basin a mile above, and since the bull wasn't too alarmed and it was warm and late in the morning, I didn't think he'd leave the trees. So I circled up the slope, above the timber and along an immense rockslide, toward the end of the forest in the basin. Above that stand of timber, I knew there was no way the bull could scent me.

I circled to the head of that stand of lodgepoles. There were no elk tracks leaving it, which meant the bull was still below in the trees. The wind was still blowing up the canyon, into my face, and still warming. I'd be able to still-hunt down into the trees without worrying that the bull might scent me. The stalking would be quiet on the new, wet snow, and any small noise I might make would be carried harmlessly away on the breeze. If the bull had bedded, and I was pretty sure he had since he wasn't too alarmed, there was a very good chance I could get up on him. Everything was perfect. I eased into the timber, the rifle in my hands just the way I'd carry a shotgun when approaching a covey of grouse, and my thumb on the safety. I tucked the sling away in my pocket so there'd be no temptation to hang the rifle from my shoulder, and so it wouldn't catch on brush and make unusual noises as I stalked down on where I hoped the bull would be.

Before long, I found the bull's tracks; they meandered through the trees. He'd circled up the slope, then circled back down. He wasn't feeding, so he must have been looking for a bed. The tracks I was following were moving into the wind, so he still wouldn't be able to scent me. I followed the trail, watching carefully ahead. I just knew he was near. Frequently, I'd sit down and stare downslope under the pine branches, looking for something that didn't quite belong. Then I saw his legs. At first they looked like sapling trunks. He was standing and suspicious. He couldn't have scented me and he hadn't seen anything, so he must have heard something. Since there were red squirrels still cutting cones from the trees, other elk, deer, and the occasional goat or bighorn sheep in that country, a sound alone wouldn't frighten an elk off unless he could associate it with man.

I scooted around a deadfall and then a pine, trying to get an open shot. When I could see the reddish mane fur where it joined the head, I centered the cross hairs at the base of the skull and pressed the trigger. The muzzle blast of the .270 in the silent confines of the big, virgin pine stand was like firing a cannon in a cathedral. When I came down out of the recoil the bull was gone, but I knew I'd gotten him. He was a fair 5 by 5 bull, though no real trophy, and he'd died instantly. I had wanted him more for my winter meat supply anyway, and I valued him a great deal for the way I had collected him.

If the winter is late in arriving, bulls will return to high country after the rut in order to get away from hunters and from competition for food from cow elk in lower country. Bulls must regain at least part of the weight they lost during the rigorous rutting or they won't survive the winter. If there's a lot of hunting pressure lower down the mountain, bulls will go high even if snows are heavy and will feed on wind-blown ridges or will eat saplings and brush. Several times I've taken good bulls up high when hunters in lowlands were having absolutely no luck. Bull elk, especially wise old veterans, have an uncanny ability to know when hunting seasons are on and when they end. A number of times I've seen good bulls in low country that had been barren of elk two days earlier while the hunt was still on.

When stalking elk late in the season, say October through December, the best tactics include tracking in snow and glassing. Elk are obvious on snow, more so in the open, and are easy to locate from a distance. At the same time, elk have good eyesight, right up there with mule deer, mountain sheep, and pronghorn antelope, so they can see you, too. Keep hidden, wear white camouflage if it's legal (though in most elk states it's not), and be careful to stay out of sight on the stalk. If there isn't enough cover to keep you hidden until you're within rifle range, consider looking for another band of elk.

Elk also have good hearing and scenting abilities, which make them difficult animals to get close to. One good thing about late-season, high-country stalking is that you'll normally be hunting on snow, and if the snow is cold and fresh, it'll muffle your sounds and

23

Alpine Mule Deer

If weather permits, big mule deer bucks will stay high until the rut in mid-November. Many trophy bucks spend the summer and early autumn in above-timberline basins over twelve thousand feet in elevation, on high and open ridges, and in the upper reaches of timber just below timberline. If it snows heavily, however, they're forced down into lower country where they can get at feed. The best time to hunt trophy mule bucks in the high country—where few hunters venture—is as early as you can. Archery seasons begin in August, but stalking close enough to stick an arrow through the chest of a wily, old mule deer is nearly as difficult as drawing a royal flush at seven-card stud. With practice, though, it can be done, and smaller bucks are much easier to skewer. Also, in some muley states, there are early firearms hunts in September in high-country areas.

During the day, the air warms, becomes less dense, and rises, so breezes normally blow uphill. Mule deer bucks that live in open basins or slopes usually bed in small pockets of short brush, thickets of pine, fir, or willow, or even tall grasses. If a buck stands up in such short vegetation, a hunter will have a shot. The archer or early season gunner must approach the buck's cover from above so the deer won't scent him. At those altitudes and in those remote basins a buck is aware that 99 percent of all danger will come from below, so most bucks bed facing downhill. They rely on eyesight and on scent carried by rising winds to detect danger below. Therefore, you'll most likely have to approach from above, though occasionally it's possible to stalk a bedded buck across the slope at the same altitude, but only if there's cover.

At high altitudes in remote country, mule deer aren't bothered much. So even the big bucks will feed in the evening and early morning in places where they can be spotted by a hunter with glasses from a distant ridge. I've found that the best way to hunt high-country bucks is to locate one as he's feeding in the early morning, wait until he beds down, wait a few more hours until he is fairly secure, and when it's clear that he's settled in, then plan your stalk. If a buck has only been bedded for a short while and he sees something that bothers him, he's more likely to get up and leave.

I'm convinced that mule deer have among the best eyesight of any North American game animal, so when planning such a stalk, staying out of sight behind ridges and rocks is of highest priority. Usually the only possible approach in open high country is from above, which generally involves a long, uphill climb behind a ridge or perhaps even in the next drainage. Once on a ridge far above, you'll have to find a way to get down within shooting distance of the buck, so it's good to plan your approach carefully when you first locate the deer.

Again, you must take care to stay out of sight, but you won't have to worry about the buck's scenting you: Since it's still going to be early enough in the day that the air will still be rising, you'll be hunting into the wind. In rocky high country, it's sometimes tough to move quietly. Rocks and gravel slide, grind against other rocks, and roll; scrubby, dried branches crack and scrape. Move as quietly as possible. As long as it's still early in the day, take your time. Because the buck won't smell you and is less likely to see you since he's watching downhill, it's most important to concentrate on keeping quiet. If a buck hears a suspicious sound from above, he'll watch for whatever made it. He may stand to look the place over, move to another bed, or take off. Then, at best, you'll have to plan a new stalk, or at worst, you'll have to give it up for the day and perhaps look elsewhere for another buck.

If you are careful and patient and realize that getting up on a buck won't be easy, this approach from above on a basin buck can be an effective tactic. I first tried it on high-country bucks in the mountains southeast of Afton, Wyoming, in the late sixties. I'd taken my backpack and hiked from the end of the forest service road in Cottonwood

Canyon to the mountains a full day's trek away. In three days, I saw in the neighborhood of twenty adult bucks in high basins and on ridges near timberline. Many of these deer were difficult to get close to from below, which at first seemed the quickest and easiest way to get to them. I tried several stalks on good bucks by coming out of the timber at the bottom of the basin and using boulders and ravines as cover to get close. It never worked; the deer either scented or saw me, then took off across the basin.

While crossing from one major drainage to another, I made my way cautiously along a blade-edged ridge of unstable, jagged boulders. It would have been no trick to step on a rock and roll it, slide between rocks, and break an ankle or leg, so I was edging along cautiously. I sat on a rock outcrop, pulled a bit of jerky out of my daypack, and stared off across a big, rugged piece of the West. I had enjoyed the scenery for half an hour, when I saw the sun glint off something six hundred yards below. I looked through binoculars to see an immense buck. He was bedded in a clump of knee-high pine tangle, staring out over the basin below without a care in the world. He was too far for a shot, so I pulled back and lay down with just my head over the top. If I could ease down a rocky chute, where I'd be in plain view if the buck looked over his shoulder, and then down a short cliff, I'd be in a tiny glacier basin just above the buck and out of sight. Then if I could make my way over the lip of that and into a jumble of bulldozer-sized boulders, I'd be within range of that old trophy buck.

The wind was good, rising up the slope and into my face, so if I was quiet enough and just a little lucky, I had a good chance. I eased through the rocks, dislodging one the size of an orange; it clattered down the hill. I was sure the buck would hear it, look up, and see me. But he didn't turn his head. So many rocks roll in that steep country that basin bucks pay no more attention to them than mountain sheep or goats do.

I made it down into the tiny glacier basin, stepped quietly and slowly from rock to rock to its edge, and looked below. The buck was still there, staring off across the basin. If I could close another hundred yards, I'd have him. The basin was facing northeast, and the sun had dropped below the ridge to my back, putting the whole east face in shadow. The air was no longer warming and rising; it was dead still. At that point in my hunting career, I didn't understand that cold air would sink and warm air would rise. I didn't know that the air was now cooling, becoming heavier, and would soon start flowing downhill, carrying my scent to the buck.

I edged on through those immense boulders. I eased around one, climbed onto another, and the buck was finally within range. I took my hat off for a gun rest, eased the .270 onto it, and found the buck in the scope. The buck stood suddenly and stared at me. I was sure he hadn't heard me, since I'd been quiet as a snake, so he must have scented me. At that moment I realized that the wind was blowing from me to him, so I hurried the shot. The 130-grain spire point punched him through the lungs a little far back, and he bounded across and then down the slope for two hundred yards before he stumbled and fell, then slid another fifty down a talus slide. He was a very big deer, with a 31-inch spread. I made camp that night and for several nights after in the timber at the throat of the basin and feasted on deer chops cooked over pine coals. That trip was one of my more memorable deer hunts, and that buck's antlers still hang on my wall.

Since that first approach-from-above stalk on high-country bucks, I've employed it at least a dozen more times on muleys, as well as on high-mountain elk, various mountain sheep, and even kudu. It's a very effective tactic if you're patient, careful, and slow.

High-country bucks sometimes bed in timber at the throats of basins and feed out into the open in the late afternoon or evening. In the morning, as it gets warm, they feed from the open basins back into timber. With these bucks, tracking may work well. If the ground isn't too rocky, you can find a buck's trail where he entered the trees and track him to his bed (see chapter 5, on stalking mule deer in timber). Since the air normally will be warming and rising during the day, you'll be tracking more or less into the wind.

Too often, though, the soil in high basins or on high ridges, even in stands of timber, may be too rocky for tracking. Then, ambushing is best. In the evening, when the air will be cooling and blowing downhill, settle across the slope from where you saw the buck disappear into the trees that morning. That way, the buck shouldn't be able to scent you when he comes out to feed. Get as far away as you can while still feeling good about your ability to hit him. The farther away you are, the less chance there is that he'll see or hear you or scent you if the wind is erratic. This tactic has worked several times for me on early hunts in the Rockies.

Once I found a good buck feeding in a basin near timberline in the Wellsville Mountains of northern Utah. I'd hiked up to the basin in the dark, and as the sun hit the tops of the peaks and colored them a rich magenta, the buck raised his head from a thicket of wind-tortured fir. His antlers went high and spread well beyond the ears. Before I could figure a way to approach, he'd gone back into the timber. I gave him

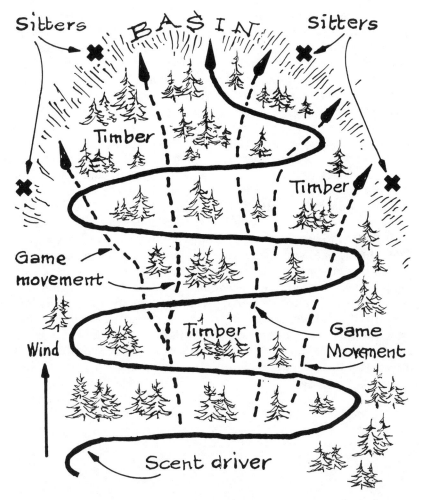

Scent driving in a high-country basin to sitters stationed above the timber.

time to settle into his bed and doze off, then I walked slowly across the slope until I found a niche in a rocky outcrop that would be out of the wind and in the sun most of the day. I waited there until almost dark. The buck minced out of the trees on the same trail he's used to enter. The shooting, as with any good stalk, was anticlimactic.

Snow occasionally forces bucks into lower country as early as even September in the high Rockies. Not infrequently, though, the snows may come late and autumn may last well into November. Then bucks will begin moving down even if there is no snow, since the rut is approaching. If Indian summer has lasted later than normal in high country, at least some adult bucks will remain. If temperatures are colder, certain browse plants will have frozen, becoming useless as feed, while sugars and starches are concentrated in others, thereby making them more desirable. Some bucks may move lower because browse plants in their basins are no longer nutritious; others with different plants in their basins may stay high. Try high first regardless, since there's a higher proportion of big bucks there and you'll have less competition from other hunters.

Stalking any mountain game requires that you be in good physical condition. Work out rigorously for at least a month before you try it, or better yet, keep on a continuous exercise program. I'm forty-three, and I do some sort of extended aerobic exercise three or four times a week, such as cross-country skiing, hiking, or snowshoeing. I also do an indoor workout, such as push-ups and sit-ups, at least twice a week during the winter, my most inactive time. In the autumn I'm always out hunting, which is exercise enough. Climbing peaks and steep ridges to get into timberline basins is tough; boning and then packing trophy bucks back down isn't easy, either. But if you're willing to accept the pain of hunting high, and you're patient and plan your stalk carefully, your chances are good of stalking up close to a trophy buck—one of the most difficult animals in North America to collect, thus one of the most desirable.

24

High-Country Caribou

Caribou may inhabit thick timber and feed on caribou moss lichen for much of the year, they may spend most of their lives on barren tundra plains, or they may live in mountains at or near timberline. Most caribou in the Far North are migratory, living on tundra flats, in forests, and on high mountains, depending on the season. Some migrate more than five hundred miles from spring to fall. They browse on several varieties of willows (important in the production of big antlers), dwarf Arctic birches, tundra lichens, mosses, grasses and sedges, and other plants.

Caribou have good eyesight, and on the plains and above timberline they rely on it. Wolves are plentiful throughout the northern wilderness, and caribou are their primary prey. A caribou knows it can outrun a wolf, and I'm fairly sure it also knows that wolves don't hunt alone so there are likely to be two or three of its friends somewhere ahead. At a distance in high country, I think caribou mistake a man for a narrow and vertical wolf as seen head-on. They will trot to a safe place and watch. If caribou are on a steep slope, they have little fear of a wolf below. In that, they're like mountain sheep. At close range, a caribou can see that a man isn't a wolf, and if it's never had experience with men before—and most of those remote-country bulls haven't—it's totally perplexed. Even downwind, a bull will rear on his hind legs like Trigger used to do in Saturday matinees and will trot off a hundred yards or so. He'll then more than likely stop, spread his legs and pee in nervousness, and stare at you. Typically, he'll circle again, frequently into the wind and scenting you all the time. Wilderness caribou sometimes act as though they've been sampling fermented lichens or hallucinogenic mushrooms, and they're often incredibly easy to shoot.

The hunting season for caribou is a long one in the very far north, opening in July and running until the following March. Caribou are hunted on the Arctic Coastal Plain in July, around Arctic Village (a tiny native village north of the Arctic Circle) nearly all year, and also in the Yukon Territory where they cross the Porcupine River above the village of Old Crow, and along the Dempster Highway (many citizens drive north out of Whitehorse for this usually annual slaughter). Not all caribou are naive and trusting of man. As such, you have to treat them with respect when stalking above timberline. They do have good eyes, and their sense of smell is as good as that of many members of the deer family.

Bull caribou normally flood the mountains of the very far north, two hundred miles north of my cabin on the Yukon River and also in caribou range well above timberline, which at that latitude is probably less than three thousand five hundred feet above sea level. One season there were incredible numbers on the summits of the highest peaks. It was and had been hot and dry, and parasitic botflies and warble flies were plentiful. They harry, hound, and terrorize caribou much of the short northern summer. The flies lay eggs in the animals' nostrils and lower backs; these eggs develop into maggots, which parasitize caribou cruelly, even killing them. If a fly finds a bull high on a rocky ridge, where caribou often go in an attempt to get away from them, the entire herd of bulls will panic and race down steep, treacherous rockslides, into the valley, over another ridge several miles away, and even into another valley. Many caribou are injured while running from flies, especially in rocks, where they frequently slice off dew claws or break legs. Once this happens, a wolf will pick up the injured caribou's scent next time the bull is in lower country and will trail him down. Without a doubt, any bull injured in such a manner is wolf feed within a week or two.

The three or four bulls I've killed in high country were taken for meat on extended three- or four-week sheep hunts. I always tried for

A caribou on typical tundra plain.

mature bulls since, before they rut, they are fat and much better eating than a rangy old cow or a yearling bull.

Stalking caribou is pretty similar to stalking any other game in high mountains. You have to use ravines, bluffs, mountains, and any other unevenness in terrain in order to stay out of sight and close the distance. Remember, caribou have good eyesight, so take the approach seriously and be careful. Keep downwind or across-wind. Caribou don't pay as much attention to sound as mule deer or elk do, but if they hear an unusual noise, they'll at least keep watch in your direction, and if you're stalking you don't want that. The goal of the stalk should be to get within range without the quarry's suspecting a thing. All animals and all regions are different, however, and a stalk pattern that works well in one place won't work as nicely somewhere else.

Mountain caribou stalking can be as classic and simple as sheep stalking. You can find a trophy bull from a great distance by glassing, first with good binoculars and then perhaps with a spotting scope to accurately judge the trophy. Then you pull off a classic, long-range sneak. The biggest caribou I've ever killed was taken just that way.

I'd found three bulls in a high basin. We'd had no meat for two weeks, since I'd killed a snowshoe hare, and were nearly out of rice, beans, and granola. If I didn't get meat within the next day or two, it would mean the end of that season's hunt. I decided to try for one of

This was my first caribou and first head of Alaskan game, bagged in 1981.

An exceptional barren-ground caribou silhouetted against the slopes of the Yukon's Ogilvie Mountains.

the caribou. Even at the great distance, one looked like a very good trophy as well.

I stalked down the ridge, keeping out of sight of the bulls even though they were a good mile away—I was taking no chances. I moved behind a high pass that dropped into a major drainage, and I continued into the head of the basin. The bulls were three-quarters of a mile below. The sun was out and heating the air, so it was rising and blowing from the bulls to me. I slid down a talus slope and into a ravine, then walked down it toward the bulls. The creek rushed through a small yet steep gorge, which kept me out of sight. The water cascading over small falls and through boulders also masked any sound I might make, enabling me to stalk quickly without worrying about making noise. Several hundred yards below, I moved up another noisy creek, further narrowing the distance. Then I climbed out of the gorge to locate the bulls.

They were just where they had been, but instead of being bedded down, they were up and grazing on the short, green tundra. I crawled to a boulder on the edge of a bluff. The bulls were grazing toward me, the wind was from downslope, and I was watching them across the slope. If I just stayed quiet, they should graze within rifle range. It happened that way, too. First they were within 250 yards, plausible rifle range on that open slope with the bulls totally unaware of me. Then they'd grazed to within 200, then 100.

I let the cross hairs of the 7mm/08 settle behind that big bull's

A wilderness camp—the best part of hunting.

shoulder as I marveled at his antlers. When I touched off, the bull leapt into the air, swapped ends, and ran full speed down the slope. His immense antlers vibrated like a tuning fork as he ran, and then he was gone. The other bulls simply stood and stared until I'd located the dead animal. He was heavily palmated up top and had extremely long points and double shovels. His meat was excellent and enabled us to stay in the peaks hunting and photographing for another two weeks, until a bear discovered our meat cache. He also chewed up those antlers. I'm glad I have several photos of that caribou, and a photo *is* a sort of trophy, too.

Even if the caribou isn't the continent's brainiest animal, a big bull is as handsome a trophy as you'll ever shoot. I still get a thrill whenever I see a fully mature bull with that white mane and beard and those sky-scraping antlers trotting across the crimson and gold tundra.

Appendix I

Cape Care
and Taxidermy

It's surprising how many skins and capes are ruined in the field and how many hunters, outfitters, and guides neglect or simply don't understand cape care.

Tom Hardesty, award-winning taxidermist and co-owner of Atcheson Taxidermy, sees plenty of damaged capes in his Butte, Montana, shop. He mentions a whitetail buck that looked as if it had suffered some particularly gruesome industrial accident — the head had been hacked off at a diagonal from the base of the neck on one side to behind the shoulder on the other. He shakes his head and clicks his tongue and tells of other atrocities as we step around piles of antlers. I wrinkle my nose at the smells of wet hide, paint, and shellac.

"One of the most common mistakes," he tells me, raising his voice against the whine of a power sander somewhere in back, "is that capes are cut too short." To ensure that the capes are plenty long, you should make the vertical cuts several inches behind the shoulder. It's better to have too much than too little.

Another common problem is improper skinning around the head or face. Tom recommends that if you haven't had experience, have someone who knows what he's doing handle the job, such as a guide or a local taxidermist. Sometimes that's not possible, especially if you're going to stay out in the bush for some time or if the weather is very warm and the cape is in danger of spoiling before you can get it to a professional. In such cases, you'll have to do the job yourself. First, make your vertical cuts *behind* the shoulder. Then cut along the back of the neck to the base of the skull. Slit down the back of the forelegs to well below the elbow joint. Next, make a Y cut from the base of the skull to each antler, then work carefully around the antler bases; it's sometimes possible to pry the hide loose from the antler or horn with a screwdriver.

Then comes the tough part: skinning out the face. If you're not familiar with what you're doing, go slowly. Peel the hide away from the antlers toward the nose, skinning carefully as you go. Skin partway up the ears and then cut them off at the base; you can finish skinning out the ears later. Be especially careful around the eyes and the preorbital glands—I usually feel with a forefinger from the outside into the corners of the eyes, under the lips, or into the nostrils to guide my skinning from the inside. The nostrils and lips are tricky—get all parts that have hair on it and then some. Skin slowly, always peeling the hide toward the nose. Once you've gotten the cape free of the skull, skin out the ears. Peel the hide on the outside of the ear upward, leaving the inside cartilage attached. Then cut through the inside lip cartilage in several places, making sure not to cut through to the hair side. Spread the cape out, leather side up, and remove as much fat and meat as possible without cutting through the leather. Again, take your time; it's better to go slow than to ruin a cape.

Another very common error hunters make is dragging a trophy across rough ground. Rocks, sagebrush, and blowdowns can wear hair or damage the hide. I have two big mule deer bucks staring down at me as I write this with bare drag marks on their shoulders. I bagged them many years ago, when I was in high school, and had dragged them to the nearest Jeep trail. To avoid damaging your trophy, load the animal on a horse or cape it out and pack the antlers and hide on your back.

Surprisingly, cutting the throat, either vertically to get the windpipe out or horizontally to bleed the animal, is still a common practice, though it's unnecessary. Don't do it. A dead animal doesn't bleed. If you're convinced you must cool the neck out, make a cut along the back of it and prop the hide open with twigs. (Cutting the neck may leave an unsightly scar on your trophy mount and cause the taxidermist extra work.)

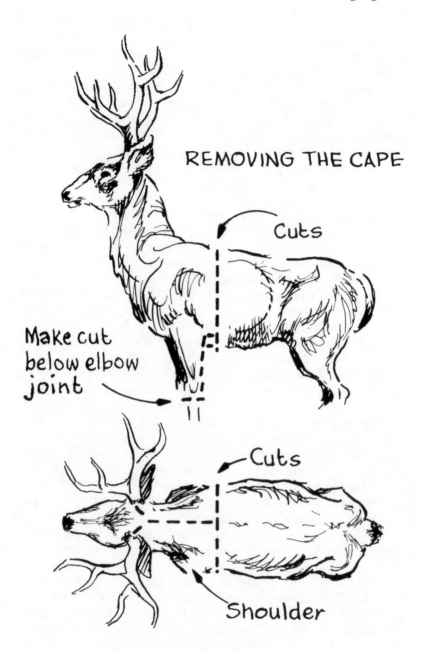

REMOVING THE CAPE

Cuts

Make cut
below elbow
joint

Cuts

Shoulder

The basic cuts for caping out a trophy head.

It's important to cool and dry the cape quickly, the sooner the better. If it's warm, as is often the case in early antelope, deer, and elk seasons, get the cape off immediately. If you don't, hair may begin slipping within hours. If there's blood on the cape, wash it off quickly. I do this as soon as I can, if possible even before caping. Otherwise I'll clean it in a creek as soon as the cape is free and before salting.

Once the cape is removed and clean, salt it thoroughly. Spread the hide out with the hair side down and layer about one-half inch of salt uniformly over the leather side. Work it into the lip slits, preorbital glands, nostrils, and other difficult places. Most taxidermists recommend noniodized salt. Let the first layer of salt stand for a day, then repeat the process with fresh salt. If the weather is wet, do the salting inside a tent. Don't store the cape in a plastic bag; it won't dry if air can't get to it. Keep the leather out of direct sunlight—ultraviolet rays will burn it. Keep the hide cool and away from heaters or campfires. Heat promotes bacterial growth and hair slippage.

The late Jim Strebel, an Ogden, Utah, taxidermist, handled my early caping attempts. He would sigh, cock his jaw a bit sideways, and roll his eyes heavenward as if asking what he had done to deserve this. Then he'd pick up my cape and shake his head sadly. I like to think I've made some progress since then.

It's common practice for a hunter to spend ten grand on a Stone sheep or twenty-five grand on an African safari only to try to save a few hundred bucks on the taxidermy. I don't understand that kind of miserliness, though I'm known to squeeze a nickel so hard it screams. If you've spent all that money on a hunt and have obtained perhaps a once-in-a-lifetime trophy, why not spend just a little more to get that trophy done by the best in the business?

Appendix II

Guides and Outfitters

Though I prefer hunting alone, and 95 percent of my trophies have been taken without a guide, there are just some places where a guide may be necessary. Canada is one of them. There I've needed a guide for hunting whitetails, moose, goats, and Stone, bighorn and Dall sheep. And in Africa, a guide is a must.

I've learned the hard way how to select a good guide. First I talk with the guide or outfitter, asking questions about the odds of success, the likelihood of getting the size trophy I want, the camp conditions, any extra expenses (in Europe and Africa there are tons of these), the actual number of hunting days (in Europe and Africa traveling days from the airport to camp are often considered hunting days), what the weather should be like at the time I'll be hunting, and so forth. As a rule, outfitters are out to sell the hunt, and a high proportion will tell you whatever they think will sell you. Many paint glowing pictures of their hunting concession, of the game, and of their guides, and much of this bears so little relationship to the truth that when you get there you wonder if you're in the right place.

My next step is to get a list of references from the outfitter, bearing in mind that he's not going to give you names of people who weren't happy with the hunt. The first question I ask these references is whether the outfitter is honest or prone to exaggeration. If all of the references tell me he's honest, then I tend to believe what the outfitter has told me about the hunt. I also ask about such things as hunting success and conditions, but if all the references tell me the outfitter is a good guy, then I know I can believe what the outfitter has told me. I always talk to at least six references. If the outfitter doesn't have that many happy clients, something's definitely wrong and you should find another outfitter.

I have found the following guides and outfitters to be outstanding, and I wouldn't hesitate to recommend them. Whenever you can, it's good to book through the guide.

GUIDES AND OUTFITTERS

Umlali Safaris (pvt.) Ltd.
Max Rosenfels (owner)
P.O. Box 19
Figtree, Zimbabwe
Africa
   This outfitter will help you get exceptional leopards, kudu, sable, and other plains game.
   [NOTE: The chief professional hunter for Umlali is Russell G. Tarr, 9 Mary Burrows Road, Ilanda, Bulawayo, Zimbabwe, Africa, ph. 67379.]

Willie Phillips, PH
Box 105
Maun, Botswana
Africa
   You can book hunts in the Okavango for a variety of species including lion, Cape buffalo, and leopards. Willie is such an outstanding guide it doesn't matter that I've had trouble with his safari company.

Ralph Kitchen
Box 843
Rossland, British Columbia
Canada VOG 1YO
   He works for a variety of outfitters and is an ace guide for Stone sheep, for Dall sheep in the Northwest Territories, and for moose.

Ken Olynyk
P.O. Box 1306
Lillooet, British Columbia
Canada V0K 1Y0

Ken does whatever is necessary to get you a California bighorn in the competitive southwest British Columbia sheep country.

Wes Vining
Safari Outfitters, Inc.
433 Yellowstone Ave.
Cody, WY 82414

I've dealt with perhaps half a dozen booking agencies, and most tell you whatever will sell the hunt. Safari Outfitters is the most reliable.

Appendix III

Guns and Calibers

So much has been written about the right caliber or gun for this species or that, and by men more knowledgeable than I on the subject, that I won't go into much detail here.

I grew up with Jack O'Connor, shooting editor of *Outdoor Life*, and was greatly influenced by him. His favorite caliber was the .270. It's also mine, and I've killed everything with it, from impalas, bushbuck, and pronghorn up to Alaskan moose, elk, and kudu. It's a medium caliber, but when used properly it can kill practically anything. (Walter "Karamojo" Bell regularly killed elephants with an even smaller caliber.)

At times, however, larger game is killed more easily with a bigger gun. For example, if I shoot a moose through the lungs with a .270, it sometimes takes the bull a few minutes to realize he's dead. So I recommend a .375 for this kind of shooting, as well as for the big African eland. In Africa, large dangerous game is legally shot only with a .375 or larger caliber. Elephants are still bagged with something over .40 caliber, and the .416 Remington has become very popular. I've used the .270 on leopards, too.

For medium game, such as deer, pronghorn, sheep, and even elk, medium calibers are good, from the .270 or .280 through the .30/06 (still one of the most popular calibers in the world), as well as the 7mm Remington Magnum, .300 Magnum, or even .338 Winchester.

Smaller calibers, for example the .257 Roberts, are often good for antelope or deer, though I wouldn't use it on elk or anything larger unless I was very close and could be certain of poking it behind a bull's ear.

Index

Note: References in italics represent illustrations or photographs